Master Your Emotions

The ultimate psychology guide on how to control your emotions, rewire your mind, reduce anxiety, stress, anger and worry. Overcome your negativity understanding emotional intelligence

Table of Contents

Introduction 1

Chapter 1: Positive Versus Negative Emotions Are Negative Emotions Really Bad? 21

    Anxiety 26

    Anger and Stress 32

    Depression 36

Chapter 2: Negative Emotions 41

Chapter 3: Dealing With Negative Emotions 47

Chapter 4: Positive Emotions 55

Chapter 5: Importance of Positive Emotions How Postive and Negative Emotions Differ 63

Chapter 6: Emotions Versus Mood The Main Differences Between Moods and Emotions 73

    How the Brain Processes Emotions 77

    Inhibitory Function 84

    Emotions and Motivation 89

Chapter 7: Influencing Emotions The physical and the Mind 93

    How the Body Influences Emotions 98

    How Thoughts Influence Emotions 104

    How Words Influence Emotions 107

Chapter 8: Changing Emotions FROM-TO Method ... 111

    Conditioning The Mind 118

Conclusion 121

Introduction

Congratulations on purchasing *Book Title* and thank you for doing so.

The following chapters will discuss

There are plenty of books on this subject on the market, thanks again for choosing this one! Every effort was made to ensure it is full of as much useful information as possible, please enjoy!

For centuries, the debate about the nature of emotions has been going strong. Some philosophers and psychologists have thought of emotions as the perception of physiological changes or cognitive decisions regarding goal satisfaction. However, with the advances in neuroscience, there have been new suggestions that the brain generates an individual's emotions by linking cognitive appraisal and bodily perception.

An example of how this may be the case is if something outstanding happens to a person one day, like getting into college. The natural response is for someone to feel happy, but what does the happiness actually lead to?

There are people who look at emotions, such as happiness, and are connected to the soul rather than the body. This is because some individuals think that the soul is what experiences the mental states, like happiness. This particular view also believes that a soul can continue to feel sensations of happiness even after a person's body is gone. However, there has been no definitive evidence that people's souls are immortal. The lack of evidence means that the above views on emotions are simply an inference.

Luckily, there are two main scientific ways that can be used to explain the nature of emotions. The cognitive appraisal theory states that emotions are judgments which connect to how a current situation matches with one's goals. For example, when a person feels the emotion happiness, that means they are evaluating whether or not their goals are being satisfied. When someone gets into college, they are fulfilling the purpose of continuing their education so that they can get a job in a particular field one day.

If a person finds themselves feeling sad, they are evaluating what their goals are, in fact, not being satisfied. Similarly, anger means that a person is aiming their judgment towards whatever they think is blocking them from being able to reach a goal.

The other scientific way to look at emotions is based on the idea that emotions are the perceptions of what is changing in a person's body. These changes can include a shift in heart rate, breathing, hormone levels, and perspiration. This view means that happiness is based on someone's physiological perception rather than judgment. Other emotions, like sadness and anger, are a person's mental reaction to different types of physiological stages.

The main issue with this view on emotions is that it does not account for the fact that bodily states are not as finely tuned as there are different emotional states. However, there is certainly some type of connection between people's emotions and the physiological changes an individual experiences.

The two scientific ways to look at emotions that were discussed allows people to gain a more unified understanding of what feelings mean. Both of the theories- cognitive appraisal and physiological perception- reason that the brain is a parallel processor, meaning the brain does multiple things at once. Furthermore, the impressions that a person experiences are both one's senses as well as their interpretations that are related to their prior knowledge.

The brain also performs emotions by interacting with both high-level judgments regarding goal-satisfaction as well as their low-level perceptions of the changes in their body. That being said, the judgments that a person has been presented through the prefrontal cortex, which interacts with both the amygdala and the insula. Both components of the brain process information related to a person's physiological state. The result is that emotions, such as happiness, can be seen as a brain process that concurrently makes appraisals and perceptions about the body.

***

A more in-depth look into some of the major theories about emotions will help further explain what emotions indeed are. Since emotions are associated with a wide range of psychological phenomena- such as personality, mood, temperament, and motivation- there are multiple theories about what emotions are.

The different theories of emotions can be grouped into three core categories: physiological, neurological, and cognitive. The physiological methods indicate that an individual's bodily response is what is responsible for their emotions. The neurological theories suggest that it is the activity within the brain that leads to a person having an emotional response. Finally, the cognitive theories propose that it is a person's thoughts and other mental activities that play a central role in emotions forming.

One of the most well-known theories of emotions was proposed by Charles Darwin. The evolutionary theory of emotion states that emotions have evolved because people have been able to adapt, which enables humans and animals to survive and reproduce. The idea is that the feelings of love and affection are what lead people to seek out mates so that they can reproduce. On the other hand, emotions such as fear force people to flee or fight when they encounter a dangerous situation.

The evolutionary theory of emotion believes that people's feelings exist because individuals serve an adaptive role. This means that emotions motivate people to react quickly to the stimuli in their environment, which also ends up helping people to improve their chances of victory and survival.

The evolutionary theory of emotion is also a relevant theory because it is vital that people understand the feelings of the other individuals and animals. This is due to the fact that being able to comprehend what another person or animal is feeling can play a crucial role in both the party's survival and safety.

For example, if a person comes face-to-face with a hissing, clawing, and spitting animal, it is likely that the person will realize quickly that the animal is frightened or feeling threatened. As a result, the person will reason that they should leave the animal alone. When a person is able to interpret someone else's display of emotions correctly, they can respond in an appropriate way that will prevent danger for both people or a person and an animal.

Another theory worth noting is one that is a prime example of a physiological approach of emotion. The James-Lange theory of emotion was developed by William James and Carl Lange, which suggests that people's feelings occur because of their physiological reactions to different events. The method interprets that when a person sees an external stimulus, that is what leads to their physiological response.

The main idea behind why this is the case is that people's emotional reaction is entirely dependent on how that same person interprets their physical response. An example of this would be if a person were walking through the woods, and they saw a black bear. It is likely that the individual will have some type of adverse physical reaction, maybe they begin to shake, or their heart rate accelerates.

According to the James-Lange theory, the person will interpret their physical reaction to seeing the bear and conclude that they are afraid. The approach also looks at the emotional response as the person is worried because they are shaking rather than the person shaking because they are scared.

The next dominant theory of emotion was created by Walter Cannon, called the Cannon-Bard theory of emotion. Cannon differed from the James-Lange theory of emotion for several reasons. One reason is that Cannon believed that people could experience physiological reactions that are linked to emotions even if that person is not actually feeling those emotions in the moment. For example, a person's heart rate can speed up because they have been exercising instead of accelerating because the person is frightened.

Another point that Cannon's theory makes is that the emotional response that a person has can occur quickly, which means the reaction cannot solely be based on their physical state. That being said, when a person encounters a dangerous situation, they will usually feel frightened before they actually start to experience the physical symptoms that are associated with being afraid. The main symptoms of fear include shaking hands, accelerated breathing, and a racing heart.

Cannon first developed his theory in the 1920s, but it was later expanded upon by Philip Bard in the 1930s. Once Bard added onto Cannon's theory, the Cannon-Bard theory of emotion stated that people feel passion and experience physiological reactions at the same time. The approach more specifically suggests that an individual's feelings are a result of their thalamus sending a message to the brain as a response to a specific stimulus. This then leads to a physiological reaction. Simultaneously, that same person's mind is receiving signals that trigger the emotional experience. The theory also suggests that since both the physical and the psychological experience happens at the same time, one does not cause the other to occur.

The Schachter-Singer Theory, or the two-factor theory of emotion, is a prime example of a cognitive theory of emotion. The theory indicates that the physiological reaction happens first. Afterward, the individual has to identify the reason behind their physiological response in order to both experiences and label the emotion they are feeling. In other words, a stimulus causes a physiological response, which is then cognitively deciphered and label as a particular emotion.

The Schachter-Singer Theory looks to both the James-Lange theory and the Cannon-Bard theory for different reasons.

Similar to the James-Lange theory, the Schachter-Singer theory suggests that individuals infer their emotions based on their physiological responses. However, the Schachter-Singer theory takes it a step further by factoring in both the situation and the cognitive interpretation that is used in order to label an emotion.

Similar to the Cannon-Bard theory, the Schachter-Singer theory believes that multiple physiological responses can lead to a wide variety of emotions. For example, if a person finds that they have sweaty palms and a racing heart when an essential exam is happening, they will most likely identify their emotions as being anxiety. However, that same person could experience a similar physical response while they are on a date with their significant other. Still, the physical reaction may lead them to believe they are experiencing emotions such as love or affection. While anxiety and love are two completely different emotions, they do have some similar physical responses.

As previously stated, the cognitive appraisal theory is another crucial concept related to emotions. The theory was created by Richard Lazarus and is sometimes referred to as Lazarus' theory of emotion. The theory suggests that thinking has to occur before a person is able to experience any type of feeling. Cognitive appraisal theory also says that the process of reaching an emotion begins with a stimulus, then a thought, and finally, the experience of a physical response and a feeling at the same time.

An example of this will be if a person encounters a giant and hairy spider. The person may have an immediate thought they are in danger of having a spider jump on them. The idea then leads to the person developing an emotional experience of fear as well as a physical reaction, which is known as the fight-or-flight response.

One final theory worth talking about is the facial feedback theory of emotion, which states that people's facial expressions have a connection to their emotional experience. Both Charles Darwin and William James touched on this idea because both men noted that there are times when an emotion is directly impacted by a physiological response instead of the response always being a consequence of an emotion.

The supporters of the facial-feedback theory believe that emotions are directly linked to the changes in facial muscles. An example of when this could be the case is if someone is forced to keep a smile on their face during a social gathering. That individual will have a better time at the event compared to someone who is frowning or portraying a more neutral facial expression at the same event.

Even though emotions impact every decision that a person makes as well as the way people see the world, there are still a lot of unknown factors related to why people have emotions. Fortunately, research is even being conducted in order to understand better how emotions affect people and what causes people to feel certain emotions in different situations.

***

Even though there are multiple theories of what emotions are, people may not be aware of why emotions are such an essential part of people's everyday life. The answer is that emotions play a significant role in how people think and behave. The feelings that individuals experience every day end up compelling them to take action as well as influence the choices they make regarding their life, both on a large scale and a small scale.

In order to truly understand how important emotions are, one must first understand the major components of an emotion. There are actually three main parts to any given emotion, the first one being the subjective component. This is how a person experiences a particular feeling. The second major component is the physiological component, which is how one's body reacts to a specific emotion. Finally, the third major element of an emotion is the expressive component. This is how a person ends up behaves in response to a given emotion.

Those three significant elements of emotions play a vital role in the function as well as the purpose behind one's emotional responses. It is also essential to keep in mind that feelings can last for different lengths of time. Some emotions are short-live, maybe someone is briefly annoyed with their co-worker, and other emotions end up being long-lasting after a lousy breakup people can be sad for an extended period of time. The differences in how long someone experiences an emotion leads to a new question: what role does an emotion play in certain situations?

One of the primary purposes of emotions is that they can help people to take action. Say a person is about to take an exam that will make-or-break their grade in a class. The person will likely feel a lot of anxiety about whether or not they will perform well on the exam and what the outcome will be if they do not get a good grade on the test.

It is because of this emotional response that the person will likely end up studying heavily for the impending exam. The idea is that since people experience particular emotions for a given situation, that leads to them being motivated to take action and make the choice of doing something positive in order to improve their chances of succeeding, in this case, to get a good grade on the exam.

People also typically take action so that they can experience more positive emotions, which leads to it being less likely that they will experience negative emotions. For example, one might search for social activities or hobbies that will give them a sense of contentment or excitement. However, this may also mean that those same people will probably attempt to avoid situations that can potentially lead to sadness or anxiety.

Another significant benefit to emotions is that they can help people to avoid danger and increase their chances of surviving as well as thriving. Darwin believed that emotions consist of adaptations that allow humans and animals to survive as well as reproduce. When people are angry, they tend to confront the source of their irritation. When a person is frightened, they will likely attempt to escape what is threatening them. Finally, when someone has feelings of love, they have a natural instinct to seek out a partner so that they can reproduce.

The overall point of why Darwin's theory also signifies importance for emotions is that emotions play an adaptive role in people's everyday life. This is because the emotions end up motivating people to act quickly as well as promote actions that will improve their odds of survival and success.

Emotions also play a significant role in people's ability to make decisions. This is due to the fact that emotions help to influence the decisions people make on a daily basis. The choices can range anywhere from deciding what to have for lunch to choosing to spend the rest of one's life with another person.

Research has been conducted, which shows that people who have certain types of brain damage end up having an alteration in their ability to experience emotions as well as a reduction in their ability to make good choices.

Even when people find themselves in situations where they think that the decisions they are making are explicitly guided by rationality, emotions still play a central role in the decision-making process. This is due to emotional intelligence or one's ability to understand as well as manage their feelings. Studies have shown that emotional intelligence plays a significant role in a person's ability to make the right decisions.

Emotions also provide people with the benefit of having other people understand them better. When people interact with someone else, it is crucial that they provide clues that will help the other person to know how one is feeling. The cues that a person offers can involve emotional expressions through alterations in their body language. This can include a shift in one's facial expressions that are connected to a particular emotion that one is experiencing in that moment.

In other instances, the cues can be a person directly telling someone how they are feeling at that moment. When someone says to their friends or family members that they are happy, anxious, sad, excited, afraid, or confused, they are actually giving other people the necessary information needed so that action can be taken.

For example, if a person goes up to their friend and tells them that they are excited about an activity that they will be doing the next day, the friend will likely take action by asking about what the activity is and joining in on the excitement for their friend. If another person tells a family member that they are anxious about a presentation, they will be giving the following day, and the family member may take action by assisting their loved on with preparing for their presentation.

Along with emotions helping other people understand one's self, emotions can also be useful in improving one's self to understand other people. Similar to how one's emotions providing others with valuable information, the emotional cues of other people can give one else the important social details needed. Since social communication is such an essential component of people's everyday lives and relationships, it requires that people are able to interpret as well as react to the emotions of other people.

Social communication through emotional expression allows people to respond in an appropriate manner so that people can build more meaningful and deeper relationships with family, friends, and loved ones. It also provides people with the opportunity to communicate more effectively for a variety of social situations, from dealing with an annoying co-worker to managing an argument between two family members.

Once again, Charles Darwin's evolutionary theory of emotions hints at the importance of understanding other people's feelings. Darwin suggested that the way in which a person displays their emotions can play a vital role in the safety and survival of both one's self and other people. For example, if a person encounters an animal that is growling, it is clear that the creature is angry or feeling defensive. The result is that the individual will back away and leave the animal alone so that both the animal and the human can avoid any possible danger.

Darwin understood that a person's emotional display would give other people the necessary information they need in order to know how they should respond in a particular situation so that everyone remains secure. Like Darwin's understanding of emotions, the above reasons about why emotions are such an important point out that emotions provide people with the opportunity to interact more meaningfully in their social interactions as well as with one's self.

***

Now that it has become clearer what emotions are and why they are so important, it is time to take a more in-depth look into how emotions can affect a person's health in both positive and negative ways. One of the primary understanding of the connection to the body, and one's feelings is that emotions send instructions to the heart, which then sends the message to the brain.

With that understanding in mind, it then becomes important for people to learn how to develop physical resilience from negative emotions so that they can take charge of their feelings. Throughout every moment of every day, there is a conversation that happens within each and every person that is actually one of the most crucial discussions everyone engages in that day. This conversation is usually subconscious and is based on the emotion-based signals going on between the heart and the brain.

The reason why this particular conversation is so vital is that the emotional signals going on between the brain and the heart ends up determining what type of chemicals are then released into a person's body.

For example, when a person is feeling negative emotions, such as anger, jealousy, or anger, the heart will send a signal to the brain that matches one's feelings. The signs end up being irregular and chaotic because the negative emotions themselves are erratic and disorganized.

Stress is one of the most well-known emotions that leads to health issues for people. This is because stress can have so many ups and downs that the body has a difficult time coping with all of the shifts in emotions that a person can experience in a short period of time.

When a person is experiencing the stress of a negative emotion, they end up having an increase in their cortisol and adrenaline levels. When these hormones, also known as stress hormones, are released into a person's bloodstream, the response is that the body prepares a powerful reaction to what is causing them stress.

The body's reaction most likely will include a redirection of blood supply from the organs that are set deep within the body to the places in the body that needs the blood supply during times of danger. Those areas include muscles and limbs, which are both used to confront a source of risk and stress or run away from what is causing a person stress. The automatic response is known as the fight-or-flight response, which allows a person to act quickly when they experience a negative emotion or situation.

Once upon a time, the fight-or-flight response was used to help people from angry bears that were trying to camp out in people's caves. When everyone's ancestors felt as though the threat was gone, their emotions and bodily functions returned back to their normal levels. This means that the fight-or-flight response was designed to be both temporary and brief.

When the response sets in, people automatically fill their bodies with the chemicals that are needed in order to respond quickly and powerfully to any given threat. The answer is all about providing people with the most significant opportunity for them to survive. When the high levels of stress chemicals kick in, people become almost superhuman.

Everyone has heard the stories about a 100-pound woman being able to lift a full-sized vehicle off the ground so that she can save her child from being pinned beneath the car. The woman would have done so without even thinking about whether or not the act of doing so would be possible. This is all because of the fight-or-flight response. The woman's automatic response sets in because of the child who would die if she did not intervene. In any case similar to the above example, the superhuman strength that a person exhibits is due to a surge in stress hormones circling throughout the body after a person has a feeling of do or die, which originates in a person's heart.

Unfortunately, those superhuman moments of strength are only present for a short period of time. During the process, the stress hormones force the shutdown of the release of other chemicals that are used to support the critical functions within the body. The chemicals that are such down include the functions that support growth and immunity. In other words, the body is only able to be in one mode at one time, either the fight-or-flight mode or the healing and growing mode.

This information further drives the point that people are not meant to live long periods of time with stress; however, many people find themselves experiencing persistent stress on a daily basis because people are basically living in a world full of anxiety.

The modern world is one that is filled with information overload, cyber-attacks, and a lack of privacy. With all of the advances in technology, life seems to be speeding up faster than people are able to comprehend. It has become inevitable that the human body feels as though it is continuously in a state of never-ending stress. Since people tend to have a difficult time seeking out a release from this particular form of stress, they end up finding themselves in an unrelenting fight-or-flight mode, and all of the consequences that are coupled with the automatic response.

If a person were to take a look around their office, classroom, or family gathering, they would most likely see that the above point is valid. It is also not that surprising that the people who have the greatest levels of stress are also the individuals who are in the most inadequate health.

Since stress has become such a significant part of the typical human experience, studies have been done to see the relationship between health issues and stress levels. The conclusion has been that with the rise in stress levels, there has also been an increase in certain health conditions such as heart disease, eating disorder, immune deficiencies, some cancers, and strokes. It is apparent that the daily stress that people experience is taking a toll on their bodies as well as their minds.

Fortunately, those same mechanisms that create and support the stress response can also be used to relieve stress in a positive manner, even when the world is in complete chaos. The act of doing so can even be done quickly as well as intentionally.

Chapter 1: Positive Versus Negative Emotions Are Negative Emotions Really Bad?

When people think about the emotions such as fear, guilt, or sadness, they tend to associate those negative emotions as being bad. However, what if people were to make a choice not to view negative emotions as bad, what would those emotions be categorized as?

The answer would be that people would be able to accept negative emotions for what they are, a part of life. Once people stop looking at negative emotions as something that is an unwanted part of life, negative emotions do not seem as bad as they used to.

However, it can then become unclear what the real difference between positive and negative emotions is. It is vital that people understand what that contrast is between the two types of feelings because avoiding negative emotions is one of the most significant obstacles that people will face in their life.

It is crucial to keep in mind that practicing positive thinking is a great strategy to utilize in order to live a happier life; however, the purpose of doing so should not be to get rid of one's negative emotions. This is partly due to the fact that people typically choose the thoughts that trigger more positive emotions, but people also benefit from feeling the negative emotions. Negative emotions provide more benefits when they are released rather than when they are suppressed or avoided.

In order for people to feel more comfortable with all of their emotions, both the positive and negative ones, they will first have to understand how positive and negative emotions actually differ from one another.

People tend to go through life trying to do whatever they can to ensure that they are experiencing positive emotions because they think that the positive emotions are what will keep them happy and healthy. However, this may not necessarily be the case because feelings themselves are energy traveling around the body.

Since emotions live within the human body, and some are actually connected to particular areas of the body, the body internally reacts a certain way when different emotions are experienced. For instance, when a person becomes so sad that they cry, their lungs will actually start convulsing. People will likely find that their chest tightens when they are angry or feel light on their feet after hearing some great news. The idea is that emotions create pure forms of energy within each individual's body.

That being said, emotions are a significant part of the overall human experience, which means both the positive and negative emotions are meant to be felt. Believe it or not, feelings themselves are harmless, and it is once people try and avoid emotions that the issues begin to set in. That is why it is so central that people learn the difference between positive and negative emotions so that they can embrace all of the emotions that life throws their way.

To start, people should be aware that emotional energy is basically neutral, meaning positive and negative emotions are really just labeling emotions as something that feels "good" versus something that feels "bad." It comes down to how someone personally interprets the different forms of energy.

For example, it is possible for people to view sadness as merely another form of energy than excitement. However, people tend to gravitate towards the energy forms that are considered "positive," so it is crucial to understand the different types of energy so that people can see "negative" emotions for what they really are, a particular form of energy.

Positive emotions can be thought of as a form of expansion. This is because the feelings that are typically viewed as positive are the ones that lead to an expansion within the physical body. If people take a moment to think about what would happen if they feel a "positive" emotion, such as happiness, excitement, or peacefulness, they may feel a flood of energy that leads to their chest opening up, their jaw relaxing. Their mouth breaks out into a smile. People may also feel the muscles throughout their body relax, and their breathing becoming more profound and slower. All of those shifts in the physical body mean a person is feeling good because they are feeling a sense of joy as they are growing and expanding.

Negative emotions, on the other hand, take on the form of contraction because these types of feelings are usually connected to fear, which is directly linked to the human's natural fight-or-flight response.

When a person comes face-to-face with a perceived threat, the fear that forms causes them to tense up and possibly stop in their tracks. This is because people are actually contracting, constricting, and preparing to fight. This can come in the form of attacking or defending one's self. The human body can be affected by the fight-or-flight response, whether the threat is present or approach, but it can also arise if the danger it merely in a person's head.

The other said to negative emotions centers around sadness, which usually originates from a person's fear of loss. This fear is typically based on a person perceiving a threat that is actually in their own head. The result is that the person will experience a level of heaviness or tightness in their chest. The negative emotions tend to feel more exhausting than the positive emotions because negative emotions end up draining people's energy because the energy is spending so much of its time "protecting" the physical body, or the mind, from a perceived threat.

Even though negative emotions are considered contractions, it is once those contractions are allowed to take place that the body and mind will eventually learn how to naturally relax and expand even when a negative emotion is present. The transition will also stop people from seeing negative emotions as something that has to be "dealt with," so that they can go away. The negative emotions that people experience need to come to the surface so that new positive emotions can be created in the process.

Anxiety

Although negative emotions do not present a danger on their own, the act of suppressing those negative emotions is what can lead to people having difficulties both mentally and physically.

Anxiety is one of the primary negative emotions that tend to be suppressed rather than dealt with. Unfortunately, anxiety is a normal part of people's lives. For example, a person may find themselves feeling anxious about an upcoming presentation or job interview.

When anxiety first sets in, people will find that their breathing and heart rate goes up, which pushes the blood flow towards their brain more so than any other part of the body. The body has a natural response, which is meant to prepare a person to face an impending intense situation.

However, if the physical response becomes too strong, the person may find that they begin to feel lightheaded or nauseous. That is why the excessive or constant state of feeling anxious can damage an individual's mental and physical health.

Anxiety disorder can occur at any point in a person's life. Yet, they usually set in by middle age, and women are more likely to develop an anxiety disorder than men. Having stressful life experiences can also lead to someone developing an anxiety disorder because their body is continuously in a state of apprehension.

There are many different types of anxiety disorder that people can develop, but the most common ones include generalized anxiety disorder. The disorder is categorized as having excessive anxiety without a logical reason for why that is the case. Some people with the disorder are still able to go about their daily life, but other people find that the disorder ends up disrupting their life to the point the illness puts barriers on their life.

Social anxiety disorder is another primary type of anxiety disorder that is defined by a person having an intense fear of social situations because of their fears of being judged or humiliated by other people. The illness may even lead to a person feeling as though they are alone and ashamed of themselves.

Post-traumatic stress disorder occurs after someone is a witness to or experiences something that is considered traumatic. The symptoms can set right after the event occurs or years after the trauma, and the episodes can be triggered without a warning.

Another type of anxiety disorder is obsessive-compulsive disorder, which means a person could feel overwhelmed by their desire to perform rituals or compulsions over and over again in order to suppress their intrusive and unwanted thoughts, which are also known as obsessions.

Some of the most common compulsions include hand-washing, counting, and checking something repeatedly. The more common obsessions that a person may have are being concerned about being clean, having aggressive impulses, or a desire for symmetry.

Phobias are another form of anxiety disorders that are based on a person having an extreme fear over a particular object or situation. The alarm will likely lead to a person attempting to avoid whatever the phobia is. Some of the more common phobias are having a fear of small spaces, a fear of heights, or a fear of spiders.

One other anxiety disorder to not is panic disorder. The illness can lead to panic attacks and sudden feelings of terror, doom, or anxiety. The most common physical symptoms are shortness of breath, chest pains, and heart palpitations.

The panic attacks can happen at any time, which may lead to people attempting to avoid any situations that could provoke a panic attack. That is why panic disorder can have a negative impact on a person's daily life.

Anyone of the disorders can have a negative impact on how a person goes about living their life. Still, anxiety can also affect components of the human body, like the central nervous system. Since anxiety and panic attacks can become long-term, it can lead to stress hormones being released to the brain on a regular basis. The result is that there is an increase in how frequent the symptoms, like dizziness, headaches, and depression, occur.

When a person finds themselves feeling anxious, their brain ends up flooding the nervous system with hormones and chemicals that are meant to help a person respond to a possible threat. Two examples of this are a rise are through a person's adrenaline or cortisol levels.

Even though the flood to the nervous system can be helpful for people when they are dealing with the occasional stressful event, the long-term exposure to stress hormones may become more harmful to a person's physical health later in life. An example of this would be if a person is exposed to cortisol in the long-term; this can be a contributing factor in someone gaining weight.

Another part of the body that anxiety can affect is the cardiovascular system since anxiety disorders can cause an extreme elevation in people's heart rate and palpitations as well as chest pain. A person may even find that they have an increased risk of heart disease and high blood pressure because of their anxiety disorder. If a person already has heart disease, their anxiety disorder can end up increasing their risk of a coronary event even more so than if they did not have an anxiety disorder.

The excretory and digestive systems are yet another part of the human body that can be negatively affected by having an anxiety disorder. The main issues that occur are stomachaches, diarrhea, nausea, and loss of appetite.

There may even be a connection between anxiety disorders and the onset of irritable bowel syndrome after a person experiences a bowel infection. Some of the central systems that are associated with irritable bowel syndrome are vomiting, constipation, or diarrhea.

Another area of the human body that can be affected by someone developing an anxiety disorder is a person's immune system. This is because anxiety can end up triggering a person's fight-or-flight response as well as release a flood of hormones and chemicals, including adrenaline, into a person's system.

When the fight-or-flight response happens in the short term, the increase in a person's pulse as well as heart rate so that their brain is able to get more oxygen. The flow of oxygen to the brain helps to prepare a person to be better equipped to handle an intense situation. The immune system could even experience a slight boost to it.

When someone experiences occasional stress, their body is able to return back to its normal functioning once the stress has passed. However, if a person finds themselves feeling anxious or stressed on a regular basis, or it lasts for an extended period of time. Their body is unable to get their body back to its normal functioning after the anxiety ends.

The result is that the person's immune system becomes weak, which leaves them more vulnerable to different viral infections. The person who experiences constant anxiety will also likely find that they are frequently ill, and the vaccines that are given to people regularly, like the flu shot, will not work as well if someone has anxiety.

The respiratory system is also negatively impacted by someone having extreme anxiety. This is mainly due to the fact that anxiety is notorious for causing a person to experience rapid and shallow breathing. If a person already experiences chronic obstructive pulmonary disease, then they could be at more of a risk of being hospitalized for any anxiety-related complications. Anxiety can also be linked to making someone's asthma symptoms worse.

There are some other physical health effects that anxiety can evoke such as headaches, insomnia, depression, muscle tension, and social isolation. Specific anxiety disorders can also have health issues unique to a particular disorder. For example, if someone has post-traumatic stress disorder, they might have is not aware that it is happening. Often times, people misplace their symptoms of stress as thinking the person is merely ill. The headache, insomnia, or diminished productivity may be due to more than just a cold; a person may actually be experiencing high levels of stress.

Similar to an illness, the symptoms of stress can affect a person's body, thoughts as well as emotions, and behavior. That is why it is so central that people learn how to recognizes the most common symptoms of stress so that they can learn how to manage their stress levels.

When stress goes untreated, it can end up contributing to why someone has health issues. The most common effects that stress can have on the body are headaches, chest and muscle pain, fatigue, difficulty sleeping, stomach pains, muscle tension, and a shift in one's sex drive.

Stress can lead to headaches that are intense and cause a lot of tension. Stress can also cause someone to experience heartburn because stress can end up increasing the making of stomach acid, which is directly linked to the development of heartburn. Stress can also lead to a person having difficulties getting pregnant because of stress effects both men and women's reproductive systems. For men, stress can lead to erectile dysfunction, and women can find that their stress drive is lower because of the fatigue they feel. Women may even find that the stress they feel leads them to have missed periods.

Stress can also have a significant impact on a person's mood in the form of anxiety, restlessness, irritability, depression, feeling overwhelmed, and a lack of motivation. Finally, stress also leads to a shift in a person's behavior. This can mean that a person finds themselves overeating or undereating, having angry outbursts, drug and alcohol abuse, a reduction in how often a person exercises, and social withdrawal.

A look at a real-life example may further drive how much of a negative impact stress can have on a person's life. Say a person is sitting in traffic and they are running late for an urgent appointment. The person is sitting in their car just watching the minutes go by while their stress level elevates more and more with every passing minute.

In actuality, their hypothalamus, which is considered the control system for the brain, sends out orders. In the case of running late for an appointment, the hypothalamus is sending the message out to release the stress hormones. The result is that the person's heart begins to race, their breath quickens, and their muscles react automatically. If the stress response fires on a day to day basis, the person's health could be at serious risk.

Depression

Just like with any one of the above emotions, depression can have a significant impact on a person's body when it goes untreated. It is often believed that depression affects a person's mental and emotional health; however, the reality is that depression can lead to health issues for a person when the depression becomes severe enough and if not treated properly.

When a person finds themselves feeling depressed, they show signs of social withdrawal, high levels of sadness, a loss of energy, and sometimes self-loathing. The negative thoughts and actions can go on for a long time to the point where it feels as though the person does not think that they will find happiness again. This thought process not only leads to someone being mentally affected but physically affected as well.

Some of the main effects that depression has on a person's body is insomnia, headaches, and fatigue. A person's body can also find themselves experiences chronic pain, inflammation, and diarrhea or constipation. Depression can also increase a person's risk of developing heart disease.

Depression can also lead to a person either gaining weight or losing weight because depression can cause someone to experience a shift in their appetite. Medical experts have even begun to associate extremely weight gain with other health issues such as diabetes or heart disease. A person being underweight can also harm a person's health by leading to difficulties with fertility and a person becoming exceedingly fatigued.

Chronic pain can occur with depression because of unexplainable aches and pains, such as joint and muscle pain or tenderness of the breasts as well as headaches. Research has been conducted, which has concluded a possible link between the symptoms of depression and a person's chronic pain worsening.

The connection between heart disease and depression is that depression can end up reducing an individual's motivation, which is used to help a person develop positive lifestyle changes. The risk of heart disease can also increase if a person already has a poor diet and lives an inactive lifestyle.

Some studies have found that depression can even be an independent factor for specific health problems. One research study that was done discovered that there is a one in five chance that someone who experiences heart failure or coronary artery disease will also have depression.

Inflammation is yet another health issue that depression can cause. Studies have indicated that both chronic stress and depression can be directly linked to inflammation as well as a shift in a person's immune system. People who have depression are thought to be more likely to develop inflammatory conditions and autoimmune disorders, including type 2 diabetes, arthritis, or irritable bowel syndrome.

Yet, it remains unclear whether depression is the cause of inflammation or if chronic inflammation leads to a person becoming more vulnerable to depression. That is why there is still more research that needs to be done in order to understand the link between depression and inflammation better.

The main sexual issues that can come about because of depression are based around a reduction in a person's libido. This means that a person will have a difficult time getting aroused, they cannot have an orgasm, or their orgasms become a less pleasurable experience.

There are also people who have found that depression has led to issues within their relationship with a significant other, which, too, can have an influence on their sexual activity.

People with depression can also find that their chronic health conditions begin to worsen when the depression is severe enough. For a person who already has a chronic health issue, they might end up finding that their symptoms are worse if they also develop depression.

It is possible that because chronic illness already causes a person to feel isolated and stressed, adding depression to the mix only exacerbates those feelings even more. Someone who suffers from depression may also have a difficult time following their treatment plan for their chronic illness, which will only lead to the symptoms of both the chronic illness and the depression, to worsen.

That is why it is so vital that someone who has depression and a chronic illness to speak with a doctor about strategies they can take to work through both of their conditions. The goal is for the person to learn how to manage both of their conditions better so that they can lead a happier and healthier life.

Difficulties with sleep are yet another issue that can arise because of depression. This can come in the form of insomnia or restless sleeping. When a person has a hard time sleeping, they will most likely become exhausted, which will then lead to the person having trouble managing both their mental and physical health.

Having trouble sleeping has also been linked to severe health problems such as diabetes, high blood pressure, weight issues, and certain types of cancers. That is yet another reason why people should look into ways for them to overcome depression and get better night's sleep in general.

One other major health issue to note that is related to depression is gastrointestinal problems. For someone who has depression, it is also common for them to report stomach and digestive issues like diarrhea, vomiting, constipation, or nausea. Some people who suffer from depression can also develop irritable bowel syndrome.

The link between depression and gastrointestinal issues is possibly due to the fact that depression changes the brain's response to encounters of stress by suppressing the activity that goes on with the hypothalamus, pituitary gland, and the adrenal glands.

Depression, stress, anxiety, and anger are all emotions that lead to significant health issues for people. Fortunately, being able to recognize the possible health issues can help a person to turn towards treatment so that they can better manage their symptoms. Furthermore, anyone of those emotions is treatable, even when they become out of control. Doctors can use multiple approaches to help people better manage their feelings, including therapy, medication, and changes in a person's lifestyle. It is also important that people turn to the best support system they have to help them work through whatever health problems they may be experiencing, either physically or mentally.

Chapter 2: Negative Emotions

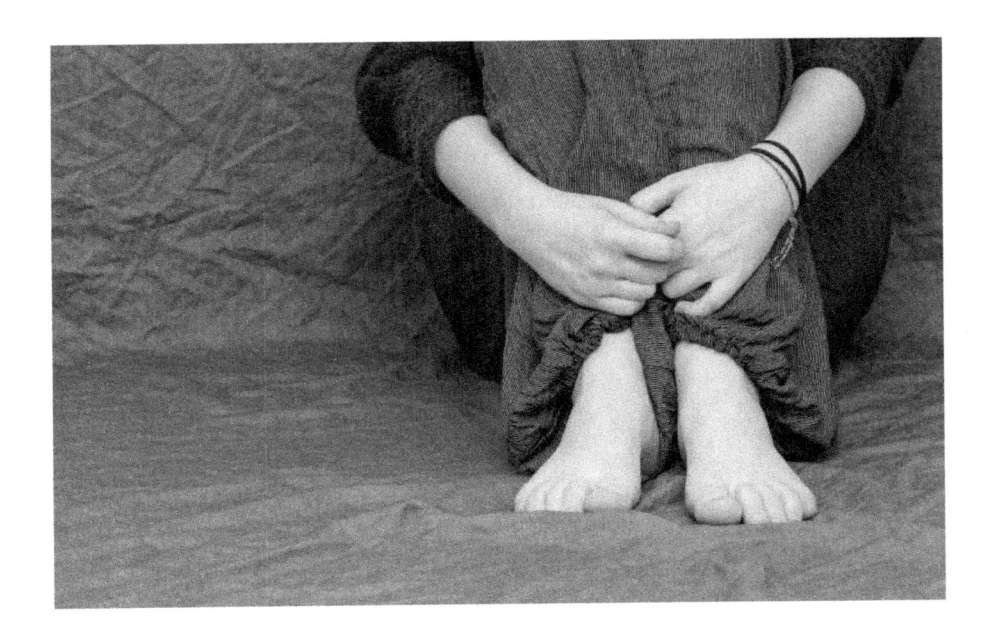

Negative emotions are a part of every person's life; however, people spend the majority of their time dealing with their negative feelings by avoiding them. Negative emotions are viewed as the emotions that cause a person to feel miserable and extremely sad. Negative emotions can even lead someone to dislike themselves or others and reduce the level of confidence they have for themselves.

Some of the most common emotions that can become negative are anger, hate, sadness, and jealousy. However, in the right setting, those feelings are actually totally natural ones. When negative emotions come out at not the best time or manner, then a person's enthusiasm for life can diminish. The best way to prevent this from happening is for a person not to let their negative emotions affect them too harshly, and they make a choice not to express their negative feelings in a poor light.

It is essential that people learn, and keep in mind, that holding onto negative emotions for too long can cause them to fall into a downward spiral. During a downward spiral, negative feelings will stop a person from being able to think and behave in a rational way. That will then lead to a person not being able to see situations in the most realistic light because they are too hung up on looking at situations the way they want to see them and remembering instances the way they want to remember them. As a result, the negative emotion, like anger or sadness, only further prevents people from enjoying their life.

The longer a downward spiral takes place, the more deep-rooted the problem ends up becoming. The same issue can arise if a person ends up dealing with their negative emotions in an inappropriate or harmful way. For example, if a person chooses to express their anger through violence, not only is this inappropriate, but it is detrimental to whoever is involved.

Also, when looking at negative emotions, it is essential to look at the overall complexity of the emotional reactions. Emotions have both a psychological and biological component because feelings are based on how a person thinks as well as how they feel. This means that everyone's brain responds to their thoughts by releasing certain chemicals and hormones, which then sends people into a state of arousal. Every emotion happens this way, whether that emotion is negative or positive.

The process is a complex one, and people typically do not have the right skills to deal with their negative emotions. This is the main reason why people find it difficult to cope with their experiences involving a negative emotion.

One way to help a person learn how to become better equipped to deal with their negative emotions is for them to divide those negative emotions into categories. The five main types of negative emotions begin with sadness, which is associated with depression, hopelessness, and despair. The second category is anxiety, which is connected to panic, worry, concern, nervousness, and fear. The next category is anger, which is linked to annoyance, irritation, frustration, and rage. The last two types are guilt and embarrassment.

Once a person is aware of the particular negative emotion they are feeling; they will then need to look into what types of automatic thoughts are causing the said emotion. After this too is accomplished, then a person could be able to really understand the feelings they are having in relation to one of the five categories.

The thoughts that are typically associated with the sadness category are self-critical thoughts, thoughts of failure or loss, and pessimistic thoughts. The main thoughts that are connected to the anxiety category are thoughts about threats, risks, or danger, what-if thoughts, and thoughts about something terrible happening in the future.

The anger category is mainly connected to the thoughts regarding the thoughts about being harmed or treated unfairly, "should" thoughts, and thinking about rules being broken. The feelings that are associated with the guilt category include thoughts about doing something that goes against one's moral, thinking about one's responsibility for possible negative outcomes, and ideas about harming someone else. Lastly, the embarrassment category contains thoughts about being judged by other people because of flaws or mistakes that a person might make.

In the majority of instances, when a person is experiencing a negative emotion, that emotion can be classified into one of the five categories above. There are also cases where a feeling can fit into more than one type of category at the same time.

Chapter 3: Dealing With Negative Emotions

After an individual learns more about what the different types of negative emotions are, it is time for them to move on to learning how to deal with negative emotions in a healthy way. However, before someone looks into ways to deal with their negative emotions, it is wise that they understand why it is crucial to deal with negative emotions so that a person is more motivated to choose to deal with those negative emotions.

When a person ignores their feelings, they are simply stuffing their emotions down instead of dealing with them in the present. This method is not healthy because the more a person suppresses their feelings, the more the feelings will fester and build until a person cannot hold the emotion in any longer.

Instead, it is better to face the negative emotion head-on because ignoring an emotion will not make it go away. The feelings may even still come out in different ways without a person realizing it because they may not be aware that they are taking their emotions out on other people. For example, if a person is angry with their significant other, but they do not want to start a fight, they might begin to take their anger out of their family and friends simply because of the anger that is present in their body from an entirely different relationship. The main reason why this happens is that people's emotions act as signals to the brain that whatever a person is doing in their life is not working at that moment.

For example, when a person is feeling angry or frustrated, the brain is signaling that something in that person's life needs to change. If the person does not change, then any situation or thought that causes the person to have uncomfortable emotions, then the person will continue to be triggered by those same thoughts and feelings in the future.

Also, as previously stated, when a person is not dealing with certain emotions that they are feeling, then that can lead to problems with their physical and emotional health. However, dwelling on anger and other uncomfortable feelings can lead to health consequences too. That is why it is so crucial for people to actually listen to their emotions and take the necessary steps so that they can let those unwanted emotions go.

Once a person is able to understand the importance of choosing to deal with all of their emotions, it is time to move on to understand what the feelings are that a person is feeling. That means people will have to look within themselves and attempt to pinpoint what situations are created the stress and negative emotions happening in the individual's life.

Negative emotions have the capacity to be triggered by different events, such as having an overwhelming amount of work to complete. Negative emotions can also be the result of a person's thoughts that surround a particular event. The way in which a person interprets what happens to them can also alter how they end up experiencing different situations, as well as whether or not those events will cause them stress.

One of the most critical roles that a person's emotions play in their life is for them to be able to see if there is a problem going on in their life so that they can figure out how to make the necessary changes.

The next step is to focus on what a person can change in their life and focus less on the aspects that are out of their control. That means that a person will have to take what they have learned from making a choice to deal with their emotions, and put it into practice. That means that people will be looking into ways for them to cut down on what triggers their stress so that they can hopefully find that they are experiencing negative emotions less often.

One of the more practical options for how someone can focus on changing what they can is for them to cut down on the stress that surfaces due to their job. This could mean that a person takes on only a certain amount of work for their career at one time or taking advantage of their vacation days during more stressful times of the year, like Christmas or Thanksgiving.

Another way to make the necessary changes in one's life is to learn how to utilize assertive communication. The goal is for an individual to stop feeling as though they are being trampled on by other people. That could mean that a person stops interacting with people who speak or act negatively towards them or learning to speak up to others when they are being treated unfairly.

One other tool worth noting is to learn how to change one's negative thought patterns by using cognitive restructuring. This method is the act of recognizing one's faulty thinking, challenging those thoughts, and ultimately changing those negative thoughts patterns into a more positive one.

After a person is able to change what they can, the next step is for them to look for the right outlet for them. Making the necessary changes within a person's life can cut back on their negative emotions; however, the changes will not eliminate their stress triggers completely. That being said, as a person changes aspects of their life in order to minimize the strength of their negative emotions, they will also probably need to find productive outlets that will help them to deal with their negative emotions.

One outlet that people commonly turn to is exercising regularly. Exercise can act as an emotional lift for people as well as be an outlet for any negative emotion that someone is experiencing.

Meditation is another helpful outlet because it can assist a person in their quest to find a sense of peace, even when they are experiencing a negative emotion. The goal is for the person to feel as though whatever negative feeling they are feeling at that moment is not as overwhelming as it once was.

Some more general outlets that can be helpful are for a person to seek out opportunities that will allow them to have fun and fill their life with more laughter. Creating more chances for a person to have uplifting moments in their life will also allow them to change their perspective on matters in their life and help relieve their stress.

The more options that a person has for positivity in their life, the less overwhelming their negative emotions will seem when they come about. It is essential to look at the healthy choices for reducing the effects that negative emotions can have on the body and the mind. It may take time to see which outlets work the best for each person, but it is worthwhile once the right ones are found.

Some other small points to keep in the back of one's mind when they are attempting to deal with any emotion includes not blowing anything out of proportion. Going over something that involves a negative emotion leads to a person going over the matter over and over in their head until the issue seems much more significant than it actually is. As a result, it seems that much more challenging to deal with the problem.

It is better for a person to learn how to be reasonable because bad feelings are sometimes unavoidable, which means it is wiser for them to think of different ways for them to make themselves feel better when those adverse feelings inevitably surface. Learning how to relax can be a great way to help a person achieve this goal. Reading, walking, or talking with a good friend are helpful ways to help a person relax when they come face-to-face with an undesired emotion.

When dealing with negative emotions, it is also important that individuals learn to notice how those negative emotions make them feel and what events are triggering the negative emotions. The goal is for a person to learn how to prepare for negative emotions in advance so that they are not as overwhelmed by the feeling.

One other point to keep in mind when someone is trying to deal with their emotions is to attempt to let go of their past. When a person continually goes over their past negative encounters, they are actually robbing themselves from living in the present because they are too caught up in feeling bad about the past.

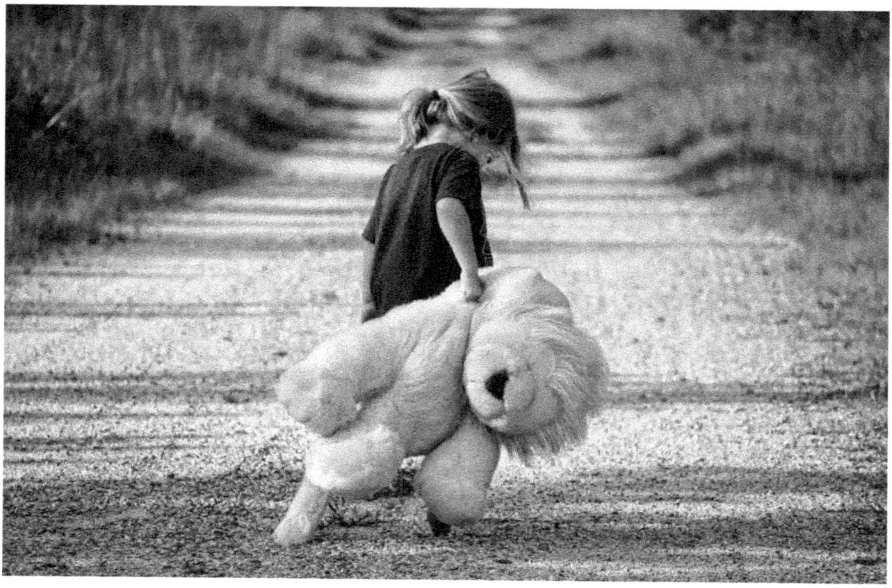

Chapter 4: Positive Emotions

There is so much attention put on negative emotions, and it sometimes even seems as though there are comparatively few positive emotions; however, this is not the case. Furthermore, psychology has spent a great deal of time looking into fixing problems that negative emotions lead to, rather than looking at the positive aspects of people's lives.

Positive emotions are the ones that are thought of as feelings that have a lack of negativity surrounding them, like having no pain or discomfort from an emotion. Studies have actually shown that in order for people to lead a healthy life, they should have a 3:1 ratio of positive emotions versus negative emotions. The most common positive emotions that have been identified include gratitude, pride, hope, amusement, joy, interest, awe, serenity, love, and inspiration. There are quite a few other positive emotions that can be considered, like the emotion a person feels when they help other people, satisfaction, or relief.

Gratitude is heavily connected to happiness because when a person is simply grateful for what they have, they are actually focusing on the positives in their life rather than putting too much weight on what they do not have.

When a person's gratitude intensifies, it not only reinforces the person's positive attitude, but it also builds upon their noble desire to help other people. A positive attitude can also help a person to reflect on their appreciation for their gratitude and how they can use their current happiness to reach even more happiness in the future.

Pride is an emotion that can have both a positive and a negative side to it. Someone who is considered prideful is also thought of as arrogant or are more concerned with themselves than other people. This means that even though a prideful person may be happy, it might be at the expense of other people.

The positive side of pride is characterized by the pride a person has in their work or their team's work. The positive form of pride is thought of as the 'purer' side of pride because it is something that is felt naturally and is not negatively looking at other people.

Hope is a proactive form of happiness. In other words, it is the pleasure that a person finds when they think about the possibility of good things happening in their future. Hope is a gateway to someone experiencing joy and other positive emotions in their future.

The positive emotion of hope is also connected to optimism, and one's natural bias towards seeing the good in circumstances, which can help people to turn unhappy situations around by putting more of their energy into thinking about how they can make a situation better.

Amusement is the emotion that happens when a person finds something funny. They could be told a joke or something unexpected happens in the natural world that causes them to see the humor in their surroundings.

Amusement is actually one of the easiest ways for a person to be able to connect with other people because sharing a laugh with someone else can help strengthen a social bond. Amusement is also useful for people who are trying not to take everything too seriously, especially with one's self. If a person is able to laugh at their own mistakes, then they can learn how to find happiness after one's lowest lows.

Another positive emotion, joy, can range anywhere from someone feeling comfortable to them being in complete bliss. Joy is probably one of the most commonly identified positive emotions, maybe because it is also one of the most sought out emotions too. However, joy is usually a short-term experience, happening quickly, but also fading just as fast.

Joy is something that can be found in many different positive emotions because positive emotions, in general, are linked to a person being happy; however, it is still helpful to separate the different positive emotions from one another so that a person can honestly know what they are experiencing in a given moment. It is even thought that happiness is increased after a person is able to find things in life that bring them joy.

Interest is the positive emotion that is used to help people meet their needs and goals in their life. This emotion is also influenced by one's curiosity about what is new around them. In a sense, interest is a form of arousal. When a person takes an interest in what is going on around them, they are also opening their eyes to the pleasures in life that they have not fully discovered yet.

Awe is the feeling a person gets when they the sun setting over the water, or they have stepped into a wholly refurbished apartment that they love. It is what a person feels when they listen to their favorite artist singing their most passionate song. The feeling of awe is one that can be experienced and appreciated through paintings, performances, and other forms of creative expression.

The feeling of being in awe is something that is also felt in a spiritual way. For example, someone could marvel at the entirety of their god or the limitless universe. When a person is feeling the emotion of being in awe, they are opening their mind and body to new experiences that will further bring them happiness because they are focusing on what is happening around them, within them, and really anything that they can feel or see.

Serenity is the feeling a person gets when they are content with what they currently have. Serenity is basically what happens when a person has a lack of pain in their life, both physically or mentally. This is partly due to the fact that serenity is linked to the spiritual state of a person feeling as though they are one with the universe rather than feeling like a victim or recipient of fate.

Love is another positive emotion that is one of the more commonly identified ones because it is a powerful emotion that is first experienced as an infant towards either one's parents or caregivers.

However, love is also an extremely complex emotion that has comes in multiple forms that are sometimes reciprocated, but other times it is not. It is believed that the purest form of love is unconditional, which means people are seeking to give without looking to receive anything in return. The romantic love that is experienced between people is one that is one that both gives and takes affection from one another.

The final most identifiable positive emotion is inspiration. This particular emotion is one that a person feels after they watch someone else accomplish something or hear someone give a fantastic speech, and as a result, the person becomes motivated to do something different for their own life.

That is why inspiration is such a strong influencer that can be extremely useful for changing people's minds. That being said, leaders are notorious for attempting to inspire other people by using charisma and the transformational style of leadership in order to persuade people to follow them.

It is crucial to understand both positive and negative emotions because both types of emotions can be used to persuade people; however, it is possible that positive emotions are the most powerful emotions in that sense. If a person is capable of offering happiness as a reward, then it quickly becomes a more effective tool than using sadness or fear as motivators.

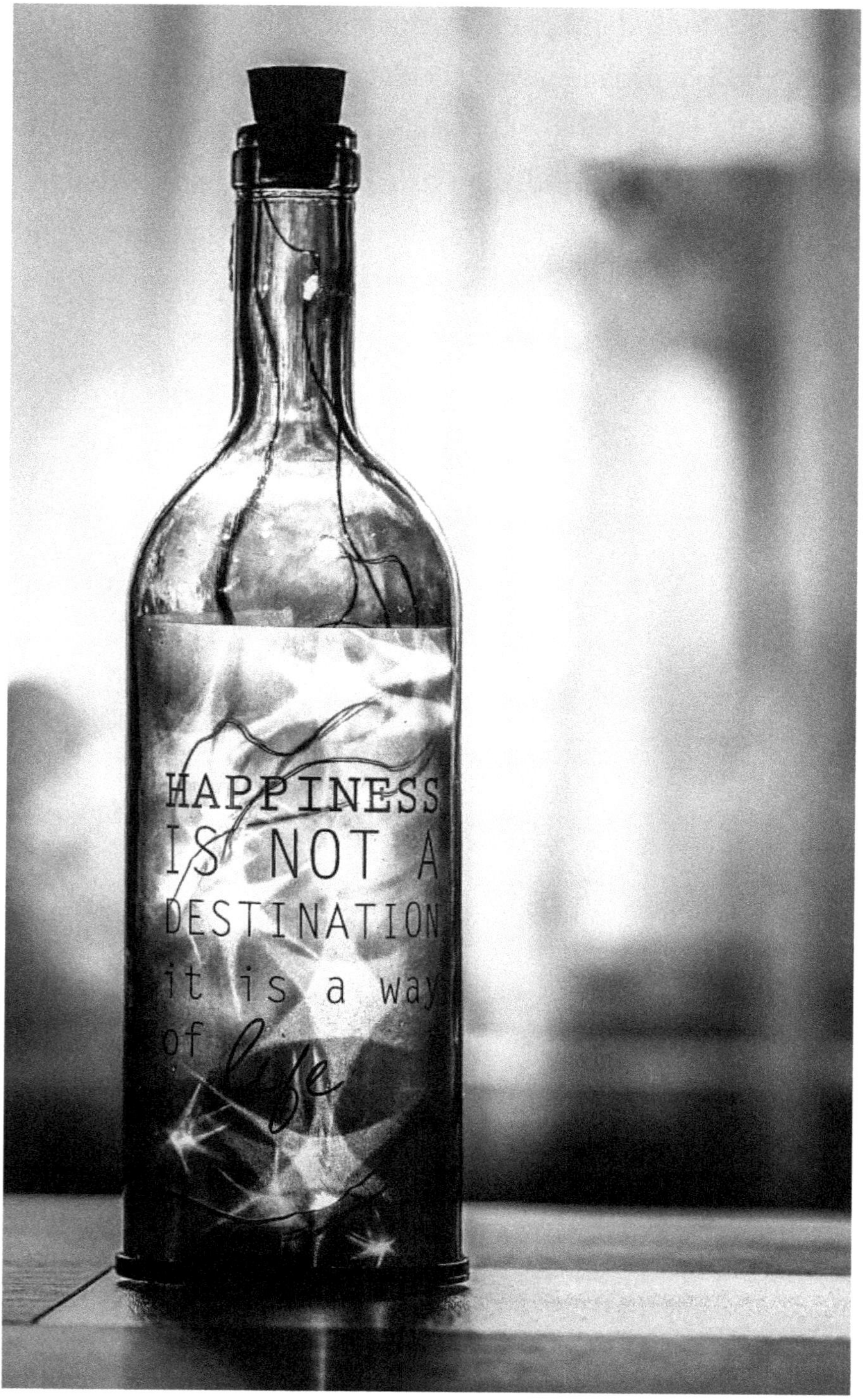
HAPPINESS
IS NOT A
DESTINATION
it is a way
of life

Chapter 5: Importance of Positive Emotions How Postive and Negative Emotions Differ

Negative emotions play a crucial role in people's survival because it is directly linked to a person's natural instinct to protect one's self and to understand what areas of a person's life need to change for the better. However, positive emotions also play a significant role in helping people to lead a happier and healthier life.

While negative emotions are the ones that tend to narrow down a person's attention or urge to one particular area, positive emotions end up doing almost the exact opposite. Positive emotions typically broaden a person's awareness and actually increases their rational thinking. In other words, positive emotions help to improve the number of thoughts people are considering when it comes to the actions they can take towards a given situation.

One way to better understand the different effects positive and negative emotions can have on a person is to compare how one's body feels when they feel a negative emotion versus how their body feels when they are experiencing a positive emotion. Say, for example, a person looks at how their body reacts to feeling sad versus feeling joyful.

When a person is feeling sad, they will often times physically look down at the ground, slump their shoulders, and not think as clearly. Mentally sadness tends to force people inwards to the point where they are oblivious to what is going on our them, or they have a slower reaction time to their surroundings. In contrast, when a person is feeling joyful, they tend to stand upright, with their chest out and think things through more rationally. The feeling of joyfulness also will likely lead to a person noticing what is going on around them and the subtle opportunities that are being presented to them. Experiencing emotions like joy will also help a person to reach out and engage with other people quicker than if they were to be feeling a negative emotion like sadness.

Positive emotions are the ones that open people up and allow them to take their surroundings in more readily. They are also the emotions that enable people to reach out to other people to connect with them, which in turn leads to stronger bonds between multiple individuals.

Studies have even found that when a person is in a positive mood, they are more creative and are more willing to come up with solutions to the problems they face in a more effective manner. Compared to when someone is experiencing a negative or neutral mood, positive moods promote more productivity in general. That is one reason why positive moods and emotions can help people in their relationships with family members, friends, and coworkers.

It is the experiencing of positive emotions that can lead to an upward spiral because the feeling of openness will ultimately lead to even greater positive emotions, which then turns into more openness. However, positive emotions go beyond being suitable for people at the moment; they can lead to long-term benefits for people too.

It is also thought that positive emotions help to build up resources for people later down the road. Emotional states may be fleeting, but they still have long-lasting positive consequences to consider. For example, positive emotions can help people get to know the world around them in new and exciting ways. When a person is feeling, say joy, they become more creative and playful. When someone is feeling interested, they tend to seek exploration so that they can learn more about other people or their surroundings. The openness that positive emotions evoke enables individuals to get to know themselves better and the world as well as other individuals in a new light. The newfound knowledge that is gained from positive emotions can help people to tackle future situations in a new and healthier way.

Positive emotions are the ones that help to build people up physically, psychologically, and socially. The people who experience more positive emotions are usually the same people who have lower blood pressure, getting better sleep, and have fewer colds. People who embrace their positive emotions are also the people who are more optimistic, accepting, and resilient compared to those who do not take advantage of their positive emotions. Positive emotions have also been known to help people strengthen their relationships because people become more focused on the good times over the negatives, like break-ups or divorces.

Human beings experience a wide range of emotions each day. Every emotion is meaningful and valuable, so it is critical that people be open to then negative emotions that happen in their life. However, it is not the negative emotions that are used to enhance a person's well-being actively or strengthen their bonds with others, and it is positive emotions that do that.

It may not always seem like the case. Still, it tends to be easier to be in tune with one's negative emotions because those are the emotions that will scream for attention, while the positive emotions are a bit quieter about their opportunities.

For example, it is apparent that a person is having an issue if there is a speeding car coming straight for them. The adverse situation will cause a person to take immediate action in order for them to protect themselves. However, a person does not have that same immediate instinct to take action when it comes to their day-to-day life.

That being said, it might be time for people to start shifting their attention away from their problems so that they can become more proactive in generating a healthier stream of their positive emotions that take place during their every life. As a result, people can become more open to themselves and connect with other people on a deeper level.

Postive Emotions and Physical Health

Not only do positive emotions help a person to improve their mental capabilities, but positive feelings can improve people's physical health as well. It is no secret that maintaining a healthy life involves having a proper diet and exercising. Still, there have been recent studies that have found a link between physical health and having a regular dose of any type of positive emotion.

There is a new study that has taken the connection between physical health and positive emotions one step further. Not only does the study show that positive emotions improve people's health, but it is able to identify how positive feelings are able to have this effect in the first place. The study concluded that positive emotions provide people with the opportunity to feel more socially connected to other individuals.

The research study divided 65 people into two separate groups. One group received training in a practice known as loving-kindness meditation, and the other group of people was placed on a waiting list to get involved in the medication training. Each participant was a faculty member at the University of North Carolina, and not a single person had any prior experience with using meditation.

The loving-kindness meditation was chosen because the practice aims to teach people how to cultivate heightened feelings of love, compassion, and overall goodwill towards other people and one's self.

The participants who were involved in the meditation group also attended a one-hour-long class every week for six weeks. During the time of the lessons, the participants were also asked to utilize some daily practices while they were at home.

Every day during the training period, as well as for two weeks before and one week after the training ended, the participants in both of the groups were asked to keep a log. The reports were meant to keep track of the amount of time they were spending on meditation, the emotions that they were feeling the strongest on a particular day, and the quality of each of their social interactions.

The researchers also focused on assessing their participants' health prior to the training being as well as after the training was completed. In order to do so, the researchers took readings of their participants" heart rate and their breathing patterns. The focus was mainly on how to measure the "tone" of a person's vagus nerve. This nerve regulates the heart rate of an individual because it acts as a link to the brain and the body.

The vagal tone has a connection to people's cardiovascular health, which is why researchers found it to be such an appropriate objective measurement for the physical wellbeing of their participants.

Compared to the people on the waiting list to meditate, the people in the loving-kindness meditation group ended up showing a more significant increase in positive emotions such as awe, gratitude, and amusement over the course of their training.

The individuals who showed a more considerable increase in their positive emotions were also much more likely to feel socially connected to other people over time. These people said that they ended up feeling closer to and more "in tune" with the other people around them. This means that the feelings of social connection to other people also said that there is a link to the improvements in their vagal tone.

The results of the study ended up offering some of the most substantial evidence that positive emotions can actually enhance a person's physical health. The study also was able to showcase that directly experiencing positive emotions by themselves is not totally enough for improving someone's physical and mental health. Instead, the main factor centers around how powerful the positive emotions are in regards to the connection a person has with other people.

The study ended up being the first one ever to show the way in which social connectedness provides the vital link that associates positive emotions with having better health. All of the findings are extremely important because they suggest that people can take the most practical and straightforward steps in order to improve one's own health. This means the result of the study should encourage people to prioritize how often they are connecting with other people, even if that simply means doing something like picking up the phone or sending someone a text message.

If a person is not able to connect with other people in a particular moment, it is possible that they will be able to achieve that connection when they refine their positive emotions on their own terms.

That means that as people experience more positive emotions throughout their life- whether it be through utilizing the loving-kindness meditation, focusing one's thoughts on positive memories, or indulging in activities that a person enjoys- they are most likely taking care of their bodies as well as their minds.

The main idea that was found from numerous studies and conversations have done pertaining to positive emotions was that they act as an "upward spiral" because positive emotions bring people better health. The cycle of positive emotions and good health then continues on because some research has found that good health also generates more positive emotions.

Some findings have stated that the recurrent experiences of positive emotions serve as a source of nutrients for the body because positive feelings ended up increasing a person's sense of social belonging. Positive emotions also give people the necessary boost they need to activate their parasympathetic health, which then leads to the opening up to even more rewarding positive emotions as well as social experiences.

Chapter 6: Emotions Versus Mood
The Main Differences Between Moods and Emotions

When it comes to dealing with the many emotions that people experience every day, people can sometimes forget or become confused about what the difference is between emotions and moods. If a person is able to understand what moods are, what emotions are, and develop a more transparent comprehension of what the difference between the two is, this can help people to learn more about themselves and others.

Luckily, the general differences between moods and emotions are pretty straightforward. Moods are usually a person's emotional feelings. Unlike emotions, moods can last for an extended period of time, maybe one or two full days.

When a person is experiencing one of their moody periods, they usually ended up feeling like they are going through different stages that are difficult to shift away from. The unhappy periods often feel like they are being brought on by various circumstances, maybe a person is experiencing pressure at work or at home, or they are having money problems.

Emotions, on the other hand, come on quickly, but go away just as fast. People usually view emotions as being either positive or negative, but that is not always the case. Emotions also tend to be more likely caused by an immediate instance; may it be something that someone else said, something that was witnessed, or a memory that a person remembers.

Emotions are also more likely to be more severe than moods and have a wider variety of options than moods. This is mainly due to the fact that there are so many different types of emotions, but moods are usually generalized as being a good mood or a bad mood.

Another main difference between moods and emotions is that something small that a person experiences can lead to a change in their feelings. In contrast, an attitude can be challenging to come out of because it can last for such a long period of time. It is also easier to shift from one mood to another because people can experience more than one emotion at the same time because emotions can reflect on different parts of a person.

Another main factor of emotions is the way in which feelings affect a person. The physical sensations that a person experiences when they have an emotion is directly connected to the effect that emotions have on a person. This can come in the form of butterflies in someone's stomach when they have anxiety, or it could be the tense muscles that come about when someone is angry. The effects of emotions can be something that is noticed about a particular feeling or the component that is the most distressing about an emotion.

It can be challenging to differentiate between moods and emotions, also because the pair can happen at the same time; however, emotions tend to stand in front of the mood. For example, when a person is in a bad mood, it is possible that they will have brief moments of happiness as well as joy.

Similarly, when a person finds themselves in a good mood, it is still a possibility that they could become sad or experience feelings of anger. Yet, it is even more likely that one's mood will end up influencing the emotion that they feel. That is why it is not necessarily a question of mood versus emotions, but rather, how the two coexist.

Just like how someone can feel an emotion that is the opposite of their mood, emotions, and moods can also be similar to one another. In that respect, one's feelings are susceptible to the mood that a person currently finds themselves in. A similarity in one's emotions and mood can also make them more likely to interpret their environment in a specific way that can end up distorting their thinking. For example, if a person is in a bad mood, it can be much easier for someone to misinterpret matters that will better reflect their bad mood.

Even though understanding moods and emotions- more specifically, the differences between the two- take a reasonable amount of time and practice, it will be beneficial in the end. This is because when a person is able to see that the frustration or anger they are feeling is not caused by the people around them, but rather the mood they were already experiencing before they walked through the door, they find it more reasonable to not blame other people for their bad mood or negative emotions.

How the Brain Processes Emotions

Similar to being able to understand the main differences between emotions and moods, it is also essential for people to be aware of how the human brain goes about processing different emotions.

Take, for example, the cliché saying, "somebody woke up on the wrong side of the bed this morning." The saying is used when someone is not showing signs of being in a good mood or portraying emotions that are characterized as negative. On the other hand, that same person could wake up the next day and feel well-rested, happy, and energized for no particular reason.

One of the main reason why this is the case is that a person's mood and their emotions act as a brief frame of mind that ends up influencing how they think about and view the world. That being said, feelings are also influenced by the events that people encounter every day, the amount of sleep a person gets, the hormones that are secreted, and even the weather outside. However, the brain also plays a crucial role in shaping a person's emotions and mood.

The limbic system, in particular, is a central factor in how a person feels. There are many regions that are fundamentally important for the function of a person's mood and emotions, which are buried deep within the most primordial components of the human brain. Those same regions of the brain are thought to have been the first to be developed within the human species.

For example, there is a surprisingly good side to a person feeling glum because it can provide people with the opportunity to sharpen their eye for detail. However, it is more so the positive emotions that help people to maintain a positive mindset. When a person is in a good mood, it ends up making them more open to new experiences, being creative, planning ahead, and adapting to the changes in their environment.

It is the limbic system that plays a significant part in the brain network involving the foundation of moods and emotions that a person experiences every day. The limbic system is the regions of the brain that work alongside one another in order to process and make sense of what is happening in the world. For example, if a person is feeling happy, their hippocampus may guild them towards the path by the water versus the path that is gloomier.

The neurotransmitters, like dopamine or serotonin, can be used as the chemical messengers, which send signals towards different parts of the human body. The regions of the brain then receive those signals, which lead to a person being able to recognize objects or situations surrounding them. The messages to the brain also provide people with the ability to assign what a person sees and experiences with an emotional value, which helps them to behave and make decisions.

The limbic system sits directly underneath the cerebrum, which is the most substantial part of the brain. The limbic system is also made up of structures, including the hippocampus, the amygdala, and the hypothalamus.

The amygdala has the primary function of attaching emotional significance to each memory and event a person experiences. Research has shown that when a person or animal's amygdala is damaged, they show signs of bizarre behavioral patterns. This can include becoming hypersexual, irrationally, aggressive, or fearless.

A rare disorder known as Kluver-Bucy Syndrome was observed in people who experienced a damaged amygdala due to inflammation of their brain. The syndrome leads people to no longer have a normal response to fear or anger, and they end up struggling to visually recognized objects. Dementia and seizures are two other main symptoms of the syndrome.

The hippocampus is the region of the brain that is responsible for reminding people what actions they should take in order to complement the mood they are currently in. For example, if a person is feeling happy, they may want to literally take a walk in the park so that they can enjoy their surroundings. If a person were to be feeling down, they might choose to walk over to a bar that they know will be playing the music that fits their current mood.

Studies have even shown that when a person has chronic stress, their hippocampus ends up shrinking. This may help to explain some of the standard features of depression, which includes having an unclear or non-specific recall of one's personal memories.

The hypothalamus is the portion of the brain that controls the hormones that are associated with a person's mood and ability to survive. The hypothalamus is also in charge of autonomic functions like breathing, heart rate, sleep, and sweating.

The limbic system also has the function of being able to regulate biological functions that line up with a person's emotions and mood, like having an accelerated heart rate or tense muscles when a person is feeling frustrated.

Since the limbic system is such a primitive part of the brain, the day-to-day decisions that a person makes tend to be more so controlled by the newer networks coordinate how a person should think and act during particular situations. The goal is for one's behavior to be able to help a person achieve their long-term goals, instead of always letting one's mood decide the actions taken.

Even though the limbic system contains multiple components that influence how a person uses their behaviors in order to match their emotions, researchers are still looking into the newer networks so that they can better understand how the brain control people's emotions. The two systems in particular that are being examined more closely are the cognitive control network and the autobiographic memory network.

The cognitive control network connects regions of the brain up so that they can coordinate the mind's attention as well as the concentration in order to complete any given task. This particular network of the brain recruits the front portion of the cingulate cortex and the dorsolateral prefrontal cortex. Those two areas of the brain specialize in unemotional and rational thought patterns.

The autobiographical memory network is used to process information that is related to one's self. A person will really only find that their autobiographic memory network turns on once they become preoccupied with thoughts surrounding one's self. This can include being able to recall personal memories or opportunities for self-reflection. The main components of this network include the areas that makeup the prefrontal cortex, which sits at the front of the brain. The main areas of the prefrontal cortex are the hippocampus, the posterior cingulate cortex, and the parietal regions that are central for a person's mental imagery.

The cognitive control network and the autobiographical memory network are thought to have a bit of a strained relationship. This is mainly due to the fact that the autobiographic memory network only sets in once a person becomes consumed with thoughts about themselves. Those thoughts then lead to the cognitive control network shutting off because the brain is no longer focused on being task-oriented. As a result, the person will find that there is a reduction in their ability to finish any task they were supposed to have completed. That is actually why daydreaming can be such a hindrance to a person's work.

Conversely, there are cases where the autobiographic memory network is not in use because the cognitive control network is in the process of gaining the necessary attention of the brain in order to complete a current task. It is in these types of cases that people use the phrase that a person is "losing themselves" in their work because they are so absorbed with the task at hand that they are not paying attention to what their body and mind need.

When the cognitive control network and the autobiographic memory network to not work correctly, that is what can lead to what is known as mood disorders. Just like how there are two main networks in the brain, there are two main types of mood disorders. The first one is depressive disorders, which are characterized by a person having their mood be persistently down. The other primary mood disorder is bipolar disorder, which there occurs when a person expresses extreme highs and equally extreme lows. The highs that a person has during bipolar disorder are also known as manic episodes, and the extreme lows are called depressive episodes.

During depressive disorders, a person's autobiographic memory network is stuck being turned on. This means that the person is forced to think far too much about themselves, which can come in the form of self-loathing, brooding, or ruminating.

At the same time, the cognitive control network is being suppressed, which leads to the person experiencing symptoms that include poor concentration, slow thinking, and indecisiveness.

The main treatment options for depressive disorders involve transcranial magnetic stimulation, which means the cognitive control network is being stimulated so that it can function better. Different medications can also be used in order to restore the normal levels of the body's neurochemicals, which assist in the communication between the two networks as well as with the limbic system.

There are many therapies that aim to empower someone who is suffering so that they can regain control of their own mood. A psychologist will typically train their patients to activate their cognitive control network. One way this is done is for the patient to challenge their negative thoughts so that they can strengthen their ability to think rationally. The act of doing this will also end up disrupting the dominance of a person's autobiographic memory network through the use of mindfulness.

Even though the brain is made up of multiple functions that all play a crucial role in how the mind is able to process the emotions and actions of them, the investigations into the brain and its ability to function alongside emotions are still being examined today.

Inhibitory Function

By the time people reach adulthood, they have developed multiple conditioned reservations when it comes to emotional display, which has also become automatic. As a result, people can feel misunderstood by others or misinterpret other people during social interactions.

However, there are cases where the conditioned inhibition happens with an emotion itself rather than the display of the emotion. It is in those types of instances that other emotions can assist the inhibitory function instead of a person's motor reflexes doing so.

The most common inhibitory emotions are shame and fear. Either one of those emotions can become conditioned to formulate with other emotions. The result is that positive emotion becomes consumed with negative feelings. For example, when a person feels excited, they can be conditioned to feel unworthy of excitement due to their shame. The same can be true for someone who experiences interest because they can become afraid of it.

When a negative emotion is coupled with a person already having a conditioned response of shame, sadness can lead them to feel depressed. If a person is scared, their conditioned reservation can lead them to believe that they are going to die.

It is for this reason that it becomes incredibly confusing for the people who tend to focus heavily on their feelings or the apparent "origins" of someone's habits. For example, if a person is already feeling awful, shameful, or fearful, this can signal a heightened state of vulnerability, which then leads to someone having an exaggerated perception of a perceived threat.

Negative emotions also are not the only emotions that are complicated feelings. The cause behind any emotion has multiple elements to it. Most individuals would agree that any feeling can originate because of a specific instance and that the person who is experiencing the emotion is aware of what is causing the said emotion. For example, a child gets excited because they hear an ice cream truck coming down the street.

However, there have been recent studies that suggest that emotions can also have an unconscious cause, which is evoked as well as manipulated without a person's knowledge. Some psychologists have concluded that there is evidence that suggests that humans do not have to be aware of the instance that leads to an effect on their mood or emotions. Scientists have even hypothesized that because humans are evolving to respond to situations faster and unconsciously, they should also be capable of reacting to any emotional event without needing to be fully aware of what the said event is. For example, a person is likely to live longer if they are able to immediately stop moving when they come face-to-face with a defensive black bear. It is not required that a person be is entirely aware of the response in order to start reacting to the situation.

A research study was done at one point, which involved measuring an individual's thoughts, feelings, and behaviors in order to determine whether there are particular emotions that can be induced without a person being aware of what is causing the emotion. The study was based on a particular theory that implied natural selection has led to humans being able to notice any specific emotion-induced information automatically.

The participants were put into three separate groups, and each group was told that there would be short flashes appearing across their computer screen. Each participant was then asked to press the letter 'R' on their keyboard if the flash appeared on the right side of their screen and the letter 'L' on the keyboard if the flash originated on the left side of their screen.

In actuality, the 'flashes' that were appearing on the screens were simply subliminal images that aimed to provoke disgust, fear, or absolutely no emotion at all. The images that flashed on the screen would appear at different speeds, which made it virtually impossible for any participant to be completely conscious of the image's presence.

In other words, any one of the participants was not aware that they saw negative images such as a growling dog or a dirty toilet as well as neutral pictures like horses or tables.

The participants also ended up undergoing three other tests that attempted to measure what type of effect the images on the computer screen would have on their thought process, their feelings, as well as their behavior.

Specifically, for the cognitive measurement, the participants had to complete word fragments. This came in the form of a variety of words that are typically used to express feelings of fear, anger, disgust, general feelings of positive emotions, general neutral

feelings, and general negative feelings.

Afterward, the participants were rated on how positive or negative their overall mood was. Their moods and emotions were captured on a 7-point scale based on how strong their feelings of disgust, satisfaction, anger, fear, shame, relief, pride, and joy was.

The behavioral measurement involved having the participants being asked to take part in either a 'scary movie test' or a 'peculiar food test.' The aim was to see, for example, if the images the participants saw would have an effect on whether or not they would want to eat something unpleasant.

When the study reached the last section, the researchers ended up asking the participants more specific questions regarding the subliminal images they saw in order to gauge how aware the participants were about the study's actual intent.

The results surprisingly ended up supporting the theory about being influenced by one's natural emotional-induced response to situations. The results of the study specifically found that the participants who only viewed the images meant to induce disgust ended up using more words associated with disgust for the word-completion section. These individuals were also more likely to describe their feelings using words that reflect disgust, and most of them chose the 'scary movie test.'

The same results ended up coming about for the people who only saw the fear-inducing images because they too were more likely to choose words that related to fear, and most of them decided the 'strange food test' over the 'scary movie test.'

The findings of the study ended up being some of the first indications that specific emotions can, in fact, be revoked without a person being aware of what is causing a feeling. Also, even though the study did not actually investigate the way in which individuals become conscious of their emotions, the researcher did come up with an additional hypothesis. The researcher's suggestion was that when a person's feelings become full-blown, people end up becoming aware of the emotion they are feeling because it is at that moment that a person is able to perceive their own actions and reactions. On the other hand, when someone's emotions are weak, they are more likely not to be able to notice the reactions and actions because they are weakly-related to their emotions.

Emotions and Motivation

Emotions and motivation are typically thought of as two completely separate physiological features that seem to be connected by a cause-and-effect type of relationship. However, it is not necessarily apparent how strong the bond between them actually is.

Motivation is a critical component of a person's emotions because the pair helps a person to decide whether or not to act on a feeling. For example, if a person encounters a wild animal that seems defensive, then the fear that a person feels in that moment and their desire to not get injured will be what motivates them to attempt to escape the dangerous situation.

Motivation is defined as a person's willingness to put in the effort that is needed in order to achieve some type of goal. One theory of motivation, the self-regulatory theory, centers around the idea that people are concerned with being able to adapt themselves in order to pursue a goal.

People typically see motivation as a tool used to stimulate a person to act or behave a certain way so that they can achieve a goal. Emotions, on the other hand, are viewed as the feelings that surface because of the motivation that drives them. However, the truth is there is so much more to the relationship between motivation and emotion.

Most psychologists think that the connection between motivation and emotions form for three reasons. The first reason is that there is an arousal of both feelings and motives, which is activated or energized through a person's behavior. The second reason for the connection between the pair is that emotions simply fit together with motives easily. The third, and final, reason why the two are believed to be connected is that it is common for the most basic of emotions to have motivational properties. For example, when a person is experiencing the emotion happiness, they tend to be motivated to achieve a better performance that day. More specifically, if a person is in a good mood, they will most likely be more motivated to study for an upcoming exam. If a person is experiencing negative emotions such as sadness, they may feel less motivated to study because it is difficult for them to concentrate.

However, the similarity between emotions and motivation that are not typically noticed is that they are both connected to energy or intensity rather than merely direction or information. That means that both emotions and motivation are more so about the experience rather than the actual material being used.

In relation to the example about studying for an exam, the emotions and motivation that the person has been more focused on the energy the individual have in order to get the studying done and less on the actual information being studied.

Another similarity between the two is emotion and motivation are more often than not linked to pressure and heat. Cognition, on the other hand, is more so connected to "coldness." One other similarity worth noting is that motivation and emotions rely on the relationship a person has with themselves, or someone else, and the environment they are in.

Many theorists are beginning to see the connection between motivation and emotions on a whole new level. Theorists are even able to explain that emotions are connected to motivation to the point where human beings are executing certain behaviors in the hopes that it will lead them to happiness as well as other positive emotions. When keeping that thought in mind, it has become more apparent that emotions can be seen as one of the rewards or punishments that a person receives when they part take in a particular behavior that is motivated by the possibility of happiness in the future.

Chapter 7: Influencing Emotions The physical and the Mind

Similar to motivation and emotions, the world, in general, also has a relationship with people's feelings. That being said, the natural emotions, like happiness, anxiety, anger, and sadness, all have a significant impact on how people feel about their own lives because emotions create color in their everyday lives.

However, emotions go even farther than that because they are able to go far beyond a person's feelings. Emotions can actually influence people in ways that are unexpected. Recent studies done by social scientists have found that the body can actually change human being's minds. The mind then goes on to influence the body. Even the words that people use in order to describe an experience they have had end up having physical consequences that can be both positive and negative.

One example of how the physical and the mind can influence one another is that love is sweet. That being said, the sugar that people are exposed to around Valentine's Day is not a coincidence. A research article that was published in January of 2014 spoke about the fact that being in love will actually make food and beverages -even the tasteless tap water- seem to be sweeter.

The findings of the article were able to illustrate that there is some level of connection to the human body for the rhetorical flourishes, such as sweetheart. There have also been researchers who have suspected that the correlation between sweetheart and love begins very early on, specifically when a baby learns how to connect their parent's love with breast milk or formula.

A second example of the connection between the physical and the mental stems from the idea that importance is substantial. For example, when a person is given a clipboard that is particularly heavy, that can lead to a person coming to the conclusion that that job candidate is more serious about a job opening compared to someone who provides a lighter clipboard.

The link between seriousness and heaviness can work the other way as well. A research article that was published in January of 2011 involved psychologists telling that there was a book that was filled with either critical information or just fluff. When the participants were asked to guess the weight of the book, they tended to think that the book was more substantial if they were told that the book had relevant information and lighter if they were told that the book only contained fluff.

On the other hand, powerlessness can also lead to heaviness. If a person is convinced that they are powerless, whether it be by writing about a vulnerable experience from their past or by putting themselves in a physically weak pose, then the person becomes more likely to feel as though the objects they hold are more substantial compared to people who do not feel powerless.

This effect that the physical has on the mental might prevent powerless people from overexerting themselves because they feel as though they are unable to control the resources around them. Influential people, on the other hand, feel as though they have complete control over every resource that they come into contact with.

Another way that the physical and the mental have a relationship is through the idea that loneliness is cold. Phrases such as "She gave me a warm greeting" or "I was frozen out of the group" make it clear that the English-language has created a link between social interactions and warmth as well as loneliness with feeling cold.

A research article that was published in 2008 had scientists provoke loneliness or the feeling of acceptance in multiple volunteers by asking the participants to remember a time when they had been either excluded or included. The researchers then asked the participants to indicate what they thought the temperature in the room currently was.

The individuals who were prompted to feel loneliness ended up guessing that the room was about 4 degrees colder than the people who were made to feel accepted — a follow-up study involved excluding and including participants in a game. The findings for the second study were that the people who were made to feel excluded were also drawn to the foods that were warm such as soup. The thought was that the individuals were attempting to warm up their bodies in order to compensate for the chill that formed due to their loneliness.

One final example of how the physical and the mental influence one another is that black-and-while can cause a person to become judgmental. The idea is that there are times when a metaphor influences a specific emotion. For example, there are studies that have found that simply holding a warm beverage can make a person conclude that the strangers they see are friendlier.

An even stranger example involves seeing information in black-and-white. Merely seeing something written in black-and-white can end up making a person's judgment of other people or situations also become more black-and-white. A research study done in 2012 found that when a person was given a moral dilemma that was printed with a black-and-white border, they were more likely to conclude a stronger judgment of either morality or immorality. When the border was either gray or more colorful, the participants became more likely to see both sides of the story.

How the Body Influences Emotions

There is also a direct link between a person's body and the emotions they are experiencing. The connection between the two actually is what allows emotions to have such a significant impact on not only an individual's mind but their body as well.

When a person is able to comprehend how powerful their emotions are thorough, they can learn how to use their feelings to help them manage their state of mind and keep their body in a healthy state. For example, are people truly aware of what they can do to the view they have on their life and the well-being of their overall health if they stop trying to suppress certain emotions? The answer is that when people take the time to address the feelings that are bothering them when the feelings are present, they can restore harmony to their mind and body. By sending the connection between a person's body and their mind, they can lead a happier and healthier life.

One example of how this is the case is through looking at the emotion love. When a person is in love, they might notice that their heart begins to race, and their palms are sweating. The reason why this happens is that there is a stimulation of the chemicals norepinephrine and adrenaline. At the same time that this is happening, the love hormone called oxytocin is released. The hormone aims to make a person feel happier and more confident while also reducing the level of pain they are feeling. As a result, a person's heart becomes healthier.

Anger, on the other hand, is directly linked to resentment, rage, and irritability. The emotion can lead to a person developing a headache, skin problems, insomnia, digestive issues, and oven heart attacks or strokes.

If anger is coupled with anxiety, anger can make the symptoms of generalized anxiety disorder even stronger. This is why it is so crucial that people do not allow their anger to monopolize one's thoughts. Instead, people should learn how to realize their feelings of anger and talk to people so that they can get their feelings of anger off of their chest and let go of their unhealthy thought patterns faster.

Depression is yet another example of how the mind and body are connected. Depression is characterized as a brain disorder that can cause a person to reach emotional suffering. The illness can increase a person's risk of developing multiple other illnesses, and it also weakens the immune system.

Depression can lead to insomnia due to the fact that people with depression struggle to get comfortable and have a lot of troubling thoughts going through their heads. The illness can also put people at a higher risk of having a heart attack and can make it more difficult for people to make decisions. Memory loss can also be a side effect of depression in some cases.

A fourth example of how the body and the mind are linked is based on the saying that people's fear is written all over their faces. When an individual is scared, their blood quite literally drains from their faces, which is why people look so pale when they are frightened. The reason behind why this occurs is because of the autonomic nervous system, which is also known as the control system for people's fight-or-flight response.

When people are triggered to feel threatened, the blood vessels stop flowing to the face and extremities so that there is more blood flow circulating to the muscles. The goal is for the body to be prepared to either fight or flee from a perceived threat.

The emotion disgust can be used to explain even further how the body and the mind are connected. When a person is disgusted by something, or sadly another person, it is actually one of the most challenging emotions for a person to gain control over. Compared to other emotions, like fear or anger, disgust will cause a person's heartbeat to slow down the right amount.

Disgust is also the emotion that can lead to a person feeling physically nauseous because there is an antipathy that is produced by disgust, which also has a lot of the same types of physiological elements that make of the human digestive system.

In order for a person to be able to avoid feeling as though there is an issue with their stomach, they should attempt to take deep breaths while also reminding themselves that it is only their emotions that are trying to control their thoughts. It is also helpful for people to do the opposite of what they are feeling because of their disgust. For example, instead of making fun of someone because of one's disgust, they should try, and they should be kind to them. By doing so, one will hopefully find that they are allowing themselves to feel more positive emotions in place of their disgust.

Another emotion that can be used to explain the link between the mind and the body is shame. Shame does have cases where it can be positive because a person is not losing any of their free will or self-esteem. However, unhealthy guilt stems from a person's past, which then becomes a part of their presence because it leads to current stress.

The result is that there is an overproduction of the primary stress hormone called cortisol. The increase in the hormone can then cause an increase in the individual's heart rate, and in severe cases, it can constrict their arteries.

In order for a person to overcome their shame, they must learn how to stop comparing themselves to other people. One of the best ways to achieve this is by becoming more confident in one's self. Another tool that can help break away from shame is to stop being so caught up in and afraid of what other people say or think about them. It is healthier for people to let other individuals do whatever they want and instead focus on remembering that it is only one's self who knows the truth. It is time to challenge one's self in the hopes of learning how to love one's self.

Pride is another emotion that links the body to the mind, and like shame, there is both a positive and a negative side. When a person is experiencing unreasonable pride, it is being built off of a person's negative thoughts about other people being together. The main issue is that this type of pride leads people to feel as though there is no one better than them.

The connection that other people have can cause a person to become stressed out, which can then lead to stomachaches, heartburn, and high blood pressure. Unfortunately, a person who is proud can end up with consequences as a result of them ignoring the potential threats that their body was hinting at.

The eighth example of how emotions and the body are linked is based on a person feeling jealous. There are people who view jealousy as a sign that the other person cares; however, once it reaches extreme levels, its emotion is too much and is even unhealthy for everyone involved. Reasonable amounts of jealousy are what a person experiences when they are concerned, or they are afraid of losing someone they love. Harmful levels of jealousy are capable of destroying hearts, families, and relationships.

The stress that comes along with jealousy leads to an increase in one's heart rate and a rise in their blood pressure. Jealousy can also lead to other symptoms that other negative emotions bring out, including a poor appetite, insomnia, stomach issues, and a significant change in a person's weight in the form of gaining weight or losing weight.

In order to prevent jealousy from getting out of hand, it is important to believe in one's partner, however corny it may seem to say so. It is also necessary for people to stop comparing themselves to other people and to not confuse their reality with make-believe.

One final example of the connection between the mind and the body is through the emotion happiness. According to Aristotle, happiness is both the purpose and meaning behind people's lives.

It is also believed that happiness coincides with good health because being happy means that people have healthier hearts, their immune systems are stronger, and they will generally live longer. Happiness is also thought to be one of the key contributors for overcoming people's stress.

One study that was published in 2015 concluded that positive well-being has a beneficial effect on people's ability to survive. This is due to the fact that a positive well-being diminishes people's risk of death by about 18% for people who are healthy and about 2% for the people who have a pre-existing disease.

It is for this reason that it is vital that people look for ways to increase their happiness. People can do so by merely hugging other people that they care about and to dress to please not only other people but one's self as well. It is also wise for people to remember that smiling can lift their spirits.

Being active is yet another great tool to increase a person's level of happiness. This can come in the form of spending more time outside, finding a new hobby, or going to the gym. Getting a good night's sleep and meditation are two other essential options to keep in mind. Once a person reaches higher levels of happiness, they will be able to enjoy their life even more.

How Thoughts Influence Emotions

When looking into emotions, it is vital to comprehend that people's thoughts affect their feelings; the feelings then affect people's actions, and their actions, in turn, affect a person's happiness.

Every day that a person wakes up in the morning, they have thoughts that originate in their subconscious mind being filtered into their conscious mind. One example of how a person's subconscious thoughts are filtered into the conscious mind is when a person's alarm goes off in the morning. A person may have thoughts such as: *Wake up; That was a good dream; I don't want to go to work today*, or *I can't wait to make money today.*

Subconscious thoughts such as the examples above will pop up without a person believing that they have any control over them. However, people are actually the ones who programmed the subconscious mind, which means people have the power to change the thoughts that float around in their subconscious mind.

The subconscious mind is programmed by people's actions as well as by the thoughts that the person typically entertains. Since a good portion of a person's subconscious is programmed by their conscious mind, this means people are capable of re-programing their subconscious mind to support their thoughts. People can even control how they would like to be thinking by altering their current thoughts and matching their actions to the new thoughts.

Even though it may seem like a tricky process to accomplish, there are a few techniques that people can utilize in order to re-program their subconscious mind to become more positive. The first option is to learn how to master positive self-talk. The practice of positive self-talk will allow a person to improve their self-esteem and help them to focus more of their energy on their strengths rather than the flaws and weaknesses they have.

Some of the best ways to help a person master positive self-talk are for them to commit to no longer rejecting and correcting the negative thoughts that are irrational. Balanced thinking is how this can be accomplished. The goal is for a person to take the time to develop rational thoughts in place of their previous irrational ones.

A person will attempt to think about a particular idea or action. While doing so, they will equally weigh in on the positives and negatives without playing into irrational thoughts that will cause the person to see a situation as catastrophic.

The final step is to fully commit to blocking out the negative thoughts, even if they are rational ones so that they can re-program positive thoughts into their subconscious mind. This will mean that the person cannot let their mind wander down a negative path.

When a person is attempting to re-program their subconscious mind, it is essential to minimize negative thoughts because negative mindsets can develop once a person allows their negative, irrational thoughts to run wild. The result is that the negative thoughts lead to a person feeling sorry for themselves, which can be challenging to break away from. It is even believed that feeling sorry for one's self is one of the worst habits that a person can adopt, and it is a complete waste of one's energy.

When people let their negative thoughts venture into their minds, they start to think irrationally, which then causes them to create a negative image about themselves in their minds. The negative thoughts, as well as self-pity, can lead to a person developing depression in some cases.

Re-programing a person's mind is such an important task because the brain is what controls people's lives. That being said, if a person's mind is negatively programmed, then they are more likely to have a negative outlook on their life.

Having a negative outlook on everything leads to people feeling sad, depressed, or negative about all aspects of their life. Those feelings of sadness can then cause people to partake in unproductive and lethargic actions. The result then becomes that the person is not happy.

On the other hand, when a person has a positively programmed mind, they have a better chance of maintaining a positive outlook on their life. Having a positive outlook on one's life provides people with the opportunity to feel happy and positive in general. If a person is feeling happy and positive, that will enhance their chances of them becoming more productive and energetic. As a result, they will become more likely to partake in any actions or activates that will deepen their happiness even more.

How Words Influence Emotions

Language is yet another part of life that can influence people's emotions. There is plenty of controversy over how to define what emotions are, but there is at least one aspect that is clear; emotions are intensely personal. A person can experience a rush of anger or a flash of annoyance. Whatever the feeling is, it belongs to one's self, and it comes as a result of one's unique set of circumstances that help them to shame the way they see the world at any given moment.

At the same time, people's emotions can also be shaped by the world around them as well as the cultural experiences they come into contact with. For example, Korea uses the word "han" to express the state of feeling both sad and hopeful at the same time.

There was a book that was published, which focuses on the collection of words from around the world, which are used to express different emotions. An article was also written in relation to the book, which spoke about how vocabulary can have an effect on a person's emotional experience.

One important topic that was noted in the article was that the way in which people think about how an emotion can end up having an effect on how they feel the emotion. One example of this can happen involves feeling homesick. At one point in time, the feeling was thought of as a fatal condition, called nostalgia, because there was an outbreak of individuals expressing their longing to be home. The feeling was so intense that people began to experience symptoms that included exhaustion and depression, as well as sores and fevers. The people who suffered from homesickness could not eat, and as a result, some of them ended up dying.

Nowadays, people look at homesickness as something that is experienced by kids who are away from their house for a night or two. It no longer appears to have any connection to death. The last documented case of nostalgia, which also resulted in death, was in 1918.

The article also goes on to discuss how homesickness was able to become less severe and why the idea of being homesick has changed since the early nineteen hundreds. The idea is that the shift happened once modernity came about. The belief is that due to the fact that people's values changed because of modernism, the actions that people were able to take changed as well. For example, people nowadays are able to travel home more efficiently, and they are able to communicate with their family members over the phone or the internet. However, it is also because of the current atmosphere that people tend to long for the comfort and reassurance that their home and loved ones provide them.

Another word that is used, which also holds a lot of meaning for people, is happiness. However, while it may not seem like the case, happiness can have a dark side to it. The article touches on the idea that happiness tends to be something that people aim for, but that may not always be a positive aspect of the emotion.

For example, picture a person who is fresh out of college and has begun their job search. This same person has envisioned themselves working for a particular company for some years now. They saw themselves climbing the latter and using their success to improve other areas of their life. They associated their happiness with being successful in one specific company.

That choice can be a dangerous one because they say that a person did not get the job at their dream company. The rejection could lead to the person thinking that the source of their happiness has disappeared. No matter what another job the person gets, even good one, they will keep in the back of their mind that they did not get the job that was supposed to lead them to their highest level happiness. As a result, the person will not embrace another position the way that they should be, and they will not get as much out of the job as they should be.

The scenario used above makes it much more understandable why the article believes that it is much healthier for people to happen upon happiness and attempt to maintain in rather than envisioning only one option for what one's happiness will stem from.

Chapter 8: Changing Emotions
FROM-TO Method

When people are attempting to understand emotions better, it is essential for them also to know how to change their feelings in order to better one's self. If a person takes the necessary steps, they can alter the way that they think and how they feel from negative to positive.

Whether is a person is a young adult who is still in the early stages of their career, or if they are a seasoned professional who is feeling the pressure of an impending deadline, it is easy for them to come into contact with emotions that cause them to become doubtful of themselves. The same can be said for people who find themselves in a tough situation where they ended up in a mental battle about overcoming their self-doubt.

In cases like those it is common for people to start second-guessing their thinking, their decisions, their actions, and their emotions. The second-guessing can end up getting in the way of people embracing their positive emotions. However, this does not mean that people have to fight their self-doubt. Instead, people should look for ways to learn how to take those moments of second-guessing and guide them towards a better place as quickly as possible.

One tool that is used in psychology is known as the FROM-TO technique. The main goal of the method is to help people move away from their negatively conditioned feelings they have developed about themselves and instead focus more so on the positive emotions that people desire.

Society had created a world that is full of contrast. There is both good and bad, high and low, rich and poor, success and failure, as well as right and wrong. This has resulted in people's brains have been wired to think the same way as society does.

However, those same contrast that society has made can be used to move individuals from where they are currently to where they want to be. Through the use of logic and emotions combined, a new internal strength can form.

The majority of people view their emotions as a part of who they are instead of like a feeling that they have control over. Yet the latter is only valid once people understand how they can divert their unwanted emotions. When this does occur, people can harness in on the power and control that they have rather than letting their emotions controlling them.

In order for a person to change a habit, they have to make a conscious decision, which will then allow them to act out a more desirable behavior. When a person is able to make a conscious decision to change a habit, they are also developing a clear understanding that emotions are not real outside of people's own minds. And so, if people decide to change their minds, that means they can improve their feelings as well.

The only obstacle that stands in people's way is not knowing the process used to alter emotions effectively. Emotions are simply energy that is in motion. This means that people's emotions are the mental energy that does not only influence behavior, but it is also involved in influencing the people that one communicates with on a daily basis. The positive emotions that people experience are ones that can drive people forward, lift them up, and propel them forward. Negative emotions, on the other hand, have the capacity to hold people back, push them backward, and lead to others telling them no.

The most considerable resistance that people will face when they are attempting to change their emotions and improving their overall state of mind is that people tend to use will power on its own in order to overcome their emotional habits that are seen as unfavorable. The main issue with using will power on its own is that it frequently leads to frustrations due to the conflicting thoughts as well as values that end up whirling around in a person's mind.

It is better for people to stop instead resisting or fight their feelings and take the emotions away from the mind so that a person is able to apply their emotions in a more logical manner. It is at this time that the FROM-TO technique is at its most beneficial state.

The method becomes a quick and easy way for a person to divert their focus away from an emotion that is unwanted or does not benefit the person. Simplicity, in general, is practical because it only takes a few minutes, and in some cases, seconds, depending on a person's unique circumstances.

This does not mean that people need to create a big dream or attempt to change the world. The goal is more so pertaining to an individual's personal world one emotional at a time. As a result, people can alter their current situation and set themselves up to have a more positive future.

This can be achieved by a person merely taking a sheet of paper and putting a line directly down the middle of the paper. Creating a word doc or PowerPoint are two other great options. On the left-hand side of the sheet, FROM is written at the top, and on the right side of the paper, TO is written at the top. Below the FROM will be the negative emotions and words. Below the TO side will be the opposite of the left-hand column, meaning that side contains the productive emotions and concepts.

Whenever a person finds themselves feeling one or multiple of the concepts from the left column, they should refer back to their FROM-TO sheet. They should do so by reading, recognizing, and accepting the emotions from the left side; however, they should then look at the counter-emotions on the right side of the sheet so that they can put more focus on the emotional habits that they desire.

By looking from the left column to the right column, a person is able to improve their power to fulfill their positive emotions. In order to improve their chances of developing a more positive mindset, people can also close their eyes for a few moments and picture themselves in a situation where they are able to apply their desired behavior. By doing so, the person will hopefully be able to see the possible positive consequences that they will have if they follow through with the desired action. An example of what the chart may look like is below.

FROM Old	TO New
Being no-one	Being special
Fear	Courage
Sad	Happy
Past	Future
Failure	Success
Lazy	Energized

The visualization of any possible positive outcome proves that imagination can be seen as a person's preview towards what is yet to come in their life. In other words, imagination can act as a motivator for a person to follow through with positive actions.

Another main component of making sure the FROM-TO plan is working at its best is for people to discover when it is the best time for them to look at their sheet. Everyone has their own way of dealing with the situations they face in life, which means people will have different times and places that are right for them to look at their FORM-TO paper. For example, some people might get the most benefits from looking at their sheets when they wake up in the morning so that they are prepared to start their day off on a good note. Other people may prefer to look at their sheet partway through their day so that they have a reminder of their positive and negative emotions they should be keeping an eye on. Finally, there are also people who will find that they get the most success from looking at their sheet before they go to sleep so that they are able to tap into their subconscious mind.

The FROM-TO method believes that people are what they do or think. That means that success is not an act, but rather a habit that must be acquired. Therefore, people should not be expecting to change their way of thinking after merely reading through their sheet one, two, or three times. It takes considerable time and a conscious effort to make the necessary changes. When a person is able to make those changes, the alterations become a part of them. Research actually has shown that it takes an average of 21 days for a person to be able to form and embed a new habit.

When an individual starts to eliminate their old habits and to replace them with new ones, they are embracing the power of changing just a single negative emotion can end up changing a person's situation for the better and it can also help a person to make the process they had been striving for.

Conditioning The Mind

If a person is looking for some other ways that they can condition their mind to start thinking more positively, there some tips they can use in order to make that a reality. The first tip is for people to release their inner negativity. This means that a person is putting more focus on gaining affirmation. The person will start to take on a different approach to their thought process consciously.

The simple way to achieve this is to start spending time calming one's mind down when they find themselves feeling stressed or distracted. The idea is to slow things down. Take some deep breaths so that the person can empty their mind of any negative thoughts. It is at that moment that the person will be ready for their positive reboot.

The second trick is for people to learn how to train their brains to turn their negatives into positives. The idea is for people to start recognizing their thoughts and hone in on the silver lining of negative situations. The first step to achieving this is for people to become aware of their thought patterns. That means that people should be paying more attention to how their thoughts are flowing.

The second step is to remind their brains to focus on their positive patterns. Rather than scrutinizing situations, people should be teaching their minds how to redirect their thoughts to search out the positives.

One other tip that people can use is to look for ways of turning away from their negative thoughts. The act of doing so involves people recognizing their negative thoughts and ask themselves what the opposite of their negative thoughts would be. This can involve a person visualizing a more positive outcome to a situation they are currently in and then thinking about what steps need to be taken in order to make the vision a reality.

It is crucial for people to also keep in mind that it is easy for them to slip into old habits. That means that people should tell themselves that they are reconditioning themselves to pair positive thoughts with positive actions. Once a person makes this transition, their brain becomes predisposed to continuing thinking and acting more positively.

Conclusion

Everyone experiences moments in their life where they are struggling to deal with negative thinking. The primary emotions that elicit a negative mental state include anxiety, worry, stress, and depression.

The negative and unsupportive, thinking patterns that people experience from time to time can end up having a significant impact on people's health, job, and relationships. However, by using techniques to practice breaking free of negativity, a person can lead a happier and healthier life.

People tend to be aware that they are generating negative thought patterns, which they, unfortunately, attempt to overcome in ineffective ways. There are people who try to make changes in their life in order to get rid of their negative thoughts. Some of the main ineffective tools used include diversions, sulking, or turning to distractions. Anyone of those choses can lead to an internal battle that is difficult to win.

When people try and use one of the ineffective strategies, they are aiming to escape their negative thoughts by numbing themselves from the pain that their intrusive thoughts cause. However, the act of doing so only works for the short term. In the long run, the negative thoughts only become worse because the problem is not being addressed and fixed at its core.

Research studies have even found that when a person is struggling, arguing, or trying to push away their unwanted thoughts, the negative emotions only become stronger.

If a person finds themselves struggling with their negative thoughts, they can attempt to tell themselves that it is possible for them to turn things around and live a more fulfilling life. The way in which a person is able to achieve a newfound fulfillment is for them to work through four key components that are meant to create a more resilient, calm, and clear mind.

The first key is for a person to recognize negative thoughts and take a step back from the negative thought patterns. Negative thought patterns can be repetitive and cause the emotions that are described as being negative.

It is once a person is able to recognize and identify the negative thought patterns that they can start to take a step back from the unwanted thoughts. The process of doing so is known as cognitive diffusion. During cognitive diffusion, people learn how to see their thoughts for what they are, thoughts. This is important because people should start to realize that their thoughts do not have to be a reality because the person has the control over their thoughts rather than the other way around.

When a person is able to separate themselves from their thoughts, they can take a step away from them and step into cognitive diffusion. As a result, people do not take their thoughts as seriously. This, in turn, means that people can choose to listen to their thoughts when they believe that the thought will be valuable to them.

It is also cognitive diffusion that teaches people to stop viewing their thoughts as being the truth. Instead, people can see their thoughts, something that passes through their minds. Some can be addressed, and other ones can be forgotten. It is each individual who chose to respond to a particular event as they see fit.

The second key is for a person to come to their senses merely. Negative thoughts tend to flow in two directions. One is dwelling on the past, and the second is worrying about one's future. Either direction that negative thoughts travel down can take the form of stress, anxiety, or any other negative emotion. The objective of negative thoughts ends up being to put all of a person's focus on either their past or their future.

As a result, they miss out on the little pleasures that come from everyday life. If a person wants to allow themselves to become more present, one way to accomplish this is to become one with their senses. This means that a person will redirect their attention away from the thoughts going on in their head and put more focus on the perceptions they make from their surroundings.

An individual can be at home, in the office, or at the park but have the same goal, to notice what is around them. The person should shy away from having a mental dialogue about what is around them and instead simply become aware of what they are experiencing. The sounds that a person hears, the scents that they smell, and the sensation of feeling the air on one's skin are all experiences that can help a person become more present in any given moment.

The third key is for a person to practice mindfulness regularly. At every person's core lives, a space that knows peace; however, as people grow up, they become more drawn into their mind- the problems they face, the goals they set, and the fears they have. It becomes easy for people to get caught up in their negative thinking, which leads to them losing touch with themselves.

Through the use of mindfulness, a person can practice waking up to a mind that is more at peace. Mindfulness can help people to build up their ability to live through their awareness of the world around them and the effects it has on their bodies.

Taking part in regular mindfulness meditation has even been known to decrease people's stress, anxiety, and depression as well as improve the functioning of their immune system. Research has also found that people become happier when they become fully present in any given moment. There is immense power in the simple practicing of mindfulness meditation.

The final key to being able to overcome negative thoughts is to create helpful questions for a person's unhelpful thoughts. There are certain types of negative thought patterns that can be tricky to deal with. These thoughts are the ones that a person will attempt to name and gain control over; however, the thoughts still manage to have a grip on them.

I a person finds themselves in that type of situation, there are tools that can be used to help them lessen the grip their negative emotions have over them. The tools are categorized as helpful questions that reduce the strength of unhelpful thoughts. The goal of the questions is to mentally question the negative thoughts that a person has so that they can change their focus.

Some of the possible questions that a person can ask themselves include asking whether or not the thought is helpful in any way is the thought true, and can the thought help the person to take effective action?

When the individual asks themselves the questions, they should then provide an honest answer back in their head. The next step is to ask one's self another set of questions that are geared towards helping them create a new and more positive focus. These questions are also the ones that will prepare the person to develop a more constructive thought process.

Some possible questions that can be asked in order to change one's focus include deciding what the truth is, what does the person actually want to feel, how can they move forward, and how can the person see their thought in a new or different light? With the use of anyone of the above questions, a person can alter their focus away from being trapped with their negative thinking and more so focused on what is going well in their life.

Thank you for making it through to the end of *Book Title*, let's hope it was informative and able to provide you with all of the tools you need to achieve your goals whatever they may be.

The next step is to

Finally, if you found this book useful in any way, a review on Amazon is always appreciated!

CPSIA information can be obtained
at www.ICGtesting.com
Printed in the USA
BVHW041919251120
594220BV00018B/614